PLEASURES AND TREASURES

# IVORY

ENDPAPERS: Stag-hunting scene from a
medieval ivory casket

O. BEIGBEDER

# IVORY

G. P. PUTNAM'S SONS
200 MADISON AVENUE NEW YORK

# Acknowledgements

The author and publishers would like to thank the authorities, directors and curators of the following museums, art galleries, libraries, treasures and collections, by whose kind permission the illustrations are reproduced: Musée d'Angers, figure 18; Musée Archéologique, Ghent, 76; Ashmolean Museum, Oxford, 83; Bayerisches Nationalmuseum, Munich, 30, 88, 91, 97, 98, 100, 101, 105, 107, 108, 126, 136; Bibliothèque Nationale Paris, 1, 60; British Museum, London, 3, 11, 14, 16, 17, 24, 26, 56, 57, 58, 65, 67, 81, 84, 96, 113, 114, 115, 116, 132; Musée Carnavalet, Paris, 128; Musée de Cluny, Paris, 15, 45, 63, 70, 78, 79, 109, 120, 125; Czartoryski Museum, Cracow, 74; Musée de Dieppe, 99, 129, 130, 131, 135; Musée de Dijon, 36; Collection Florange, Paris, 117; Palais de Fontainebleau, 124; Abbey of Herlufsholm, 23; Prince Hohenlohe Collection, Schloss Neuenstein, 93; Institut Royal du Patrimonie Artistique, Brussels, 69, 111; Museum des Kunsthandwerks, Leipzig, 102, 103; Kunsthistorisches Museum, Vienna, 37, 110; Musée du Louvre, Paris, 4, 7, 9, 10, 12, 13, 19, 27, 32, 39, 40, 41, 54, 55, 59, 68, 72, 73, 75, 77, 87, 89, 118, 121, 127; Musée de la Marine, Paris, 134; Chiesa Metropolitana, Ravenna, 8; Palazzo Pitti, Florence, 112; Public Museum, Liverpool, 46; Musée de Saint-Germain-en-Laye, 2; Church of Saint-Martin-du-Bois, 104; Sens Cathedral, 5; Staatliche Museen, Berlin: Skulpturenabteilung, 94, 95 — Kunstgewerbemuseum, 106, 123; Victoria and Albert Museum, London, 6, 20, 21, 22, 25, 29, 31, 33, 34, 35, 38, 43, 44, 48, 49, 50, 51, 52, 53, 61, 62, 66, 80, 82, 85, 86, 90, 119, 122, 133; Prince Wallerstein-Oettingen Collection, Maihingen, 28, 42; Wallace Collection, London (Crown Copyright), 64, 92.

Photographs were obtained from the following photographic archives and photographers: A.C.L., Brussels, figure 111; Fratelli Alinari, 8, 112; Archives Photographiques, 1, 2, 4, 5, 7, 10, 12, 13, 19, 27, 28, 32, 36, 37, 39, 40, 41, 42, 45, 46, 54, 55, 59, 63, 68, 69, 71, 72, 73, 74, 75, 76, 77, 78, 79, 83, 87, 89, 104, 109, 118, 120, 121, 124; Bulloz, 128; Courtauld Institute of Art, 47; Delacroix, Dieppe, 99, 129, 130, 131, 135; Reinhard Friedrich, 94, 95; Giraudon, 15, 18, 23, 70, 117, 125, 127; Sophie-Renate Gnamm, 91, 98, 126, 136; K. H. Müller, 102, 103; Walter Steinkopf, 106, 123; Victoria and Albert Museum, 9; Derrick Witty, 20, 21, 25, 29, 31, 49, 52, 53, 61, 62, 65, 66, 67, 84, 85, 86, 90, 119, 122, 133.

Printed in Germany by K. G. Lohse, Graphischer Grossbetrieb OHG, Frankfurt-am-Main
Library of Congress Catalog Card Number 64-16768

# Contents

# CHAPTER ONE

# Early Ivories

MOST OF THE GREAT CULTURES of the world have known
and practised the art of ivory carving: some (like those of
India and China) from very remote times, others (like those
of Japan or America) more recently, but no less brilliantly —
witness the Japanese *netsuke*. But Europe has produced so
many works of significance in this field at every stage of its
history that there is little doubt that a survey of ivory carving affords as complete and precise a reflection of the
essential aims of western culture at all periods, as a survey
of ceramics would yield for the culture of the Far East.
Although one must recognize its debt to the Middle East,
where much of its character was formed, European production of works in ivory from prehistoric times to the
eighteenth century was consistently of great importance and
high quality.

Objects made of ivory first appeared during the Aurigna-
cian period, 20,000 years before our era; they were made
from mammoth tusks and show outstanding quality, comparable to that of contemporary frescoes, the most famous of
which are at Lascaux. It seems that their production coin-
cided with a warmer period, the post-glacial era, and the
appearance of a new and more evolved race.

These artifacts are found all over Europe, from Russia to
the Atlantic, but the most perfect of them have been discovered in south-western France. These can already be seen

1 *(opposite)* The cover of a Gospel from Metz,
an ivory plaque (9th—10th century)
embellished with jewels, enamel and silver

7

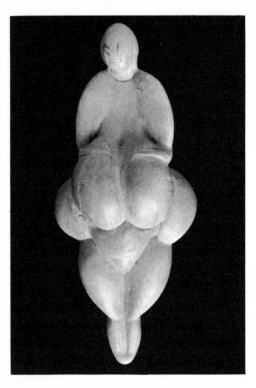

2 The human model is no longer recognizable in this prehistoric Venus from Lespugne. This amulet was intended to increase the fertility of the cave-dwellers

to exemplify the three different functions which western ivories have fulfilled throughout their history: the religious (or magical), the utilitarian, and the purely plastic.

At Brassempouy (Landes), alongside a well-shaped hand-pick with scratched decoration (a utilitarian object), a pendant was discovered with a pattern of triple wavy lines (all ornamentation must have had a magical significance) and, lastly, the bust of a woman with her hair indicated by a rough criss-cross pattern. This already, perhaps, ranks as a portrait to which one can attribute a plastic value. Thus human representations appeared from the first.

One extremely important class of objects raises far-reaching questions: a group of works of probably even greater antiquity known as 'steatopygous Venuses'. These enigmatic figures are found all over Europe – not always of ivory, it is true – and it has been suggested that they may owe something to African influence. The most remarkable for purity of line is the ivory Venus discovered at Lespugne (Haute-Garonne) [figure 2]. The adipose masses, concentrically arranged, have a magical significance; the artist has tried to express and promote the idea of fecundity, of reproduction. In the same way, most of the women and female animals in the frescoes are shown pregnant.

The idea of reproduction was one of major importance at a time when the fate of the race was at stake, confronted as it was with the multiplication of animal species. That is why in these female figures the facial features are suppressed and the sexual characteristics emphasized.

We find symbols of fecundity again featured during the Magdalenian period, this time in the form of key patterns and chevrons on a personal ornament, a bracelet from Mezin (Ukraine). These symbols are in fact found on some female figures. If we insist on the significance of the decoration of these ancient objects it is because, throughout the history of ivory, carvers sought to express themselves by means of symbols, and it is rarely that the subjects ornamenting their

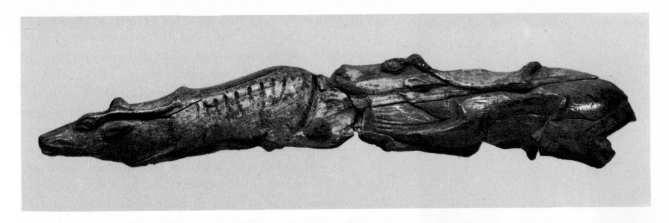

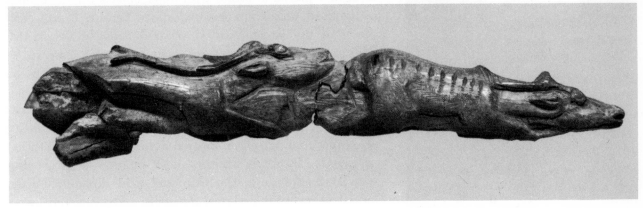

creations cannot be thus interpreted. For example, two famous groups of reindeer, most powerfully and beautifully depicted with their legs bent in frenzied flight (one in the British Museum [figure 3] and the other in the museum at Saint-Germain-en-Laye), were once in fact part of a single object: a spear-thrower, an offensive weapon. The representation of victims in flight has always had a magical significance, for it was believed that if the tool bore a picture of the hunted prey it would be more effective.

The next flowering of ivory carving was to occur at the eastern end of the Mediterranean basin, where the most brilliant advances in the art were to take place. First in

3 These dynamic reindeer, carved of mammoth ivory, were part of a prehistoric spear-thrower

4 The Egyptians' astonishing sense of composition and bas-relief is evident in this knife-handle (*c* 3000 BC)

Egypt, which excelled in utilitarian objects, much later in Mesopotamia-Phoenicia, whose decorative artifacts have a more purely plastic value, and lastly in Greece, where the emphasis was to be on the religious.

Egyptian production between the eighth and fourth millenniums was so rich and varied that it might be said to carry on the torch from prehistoric times, and as in the case of prehistoric artifacts, the earliest are by no means the least beautiful and significant. Fertility charms took on a new function — a funerary one, needless to say — since this was the Egyptians' essential preoccupation; 'concubines of death', or figures placed in tombs with other objects for the benefit of the dead, date from the predynastic period. The masterpieces of this archaic art are shared between the British Museum, where one may see a statuette of a king in an ornate robe [figure 11], and the Louvre, which possesses the astonishing knife-handle from Djebel-el-Arak [figure 4]. The arrangement of juxtaposed scenes found in later basreliefs and frescoes, their sober elegance of line and clarity of composition, are all prefigured in this object; the selection of scenes — hunting, fishing, and warfare — is in keeping with its function (as in the Bruniquel spear-thrower), for the knife was certainly designed for use in all three activities.

Innumerable statuettes have been found at Quibell, Hierakonpolis and Abydos. Later on, in historic times, Egypt was to produce excellent work of a no less utilitarian but extremely varied sort, carried out either in wood or bronze. In the remarkable ivory objects, richly pigmented, to be seen in the Caernarvon Collection at the Metropolitan Museum, New York, one can always discover the adaptation of the subject to its purpose. Whips, for instance, are normally used to control horses, and the galloping horse on the whip handle has the same explanation as the Bruniquel reindeer; whereas the graceful gazelle moving through a flowery meadow has always been likened to a charming woman, particularly in the Bible, and it is thus natural that this should be the image decorating the handle of a mirror used in feminine toilet.

Egyptian ivories attained a quality which has scarcely been surpassed. Ivories of Mesopotamian or Phoenician provenance seldom rival them aesthetically, but they are more important historically because, thanks to the fact that the Phoenicians traded all over the Mediterranean basin, we find them, or imitations of them, as far afield as Spain. The discoveries at Chiusi, in central Italy, show the part they played in the cradle of Etruscan culture, while the persistence of their tradition in Crete and Ionia was to influence Greek culture. While the Egyptians excelled at sculpture in the round, in the Phoenician ivories the bas-relief came into its own. For a long time this was to be the essential form taken by ivories, manifested in plaques for caskets, furniture and boxes of various sorts, or tubes to contain a rolled papyrus, on which Egyptian themes predominated.

Again, it is in the Louvre and the British Museum that the most beautiful examples are to be found. In London we have the curious head of an official (2500 BC), in Paris the Ras-Shamra casket-lid from Syria (1500 BC). Here we see a new variation on the theme of the fertility-goddess, still exhibiting opulent charms, and suckling two goats. Also of Phoenician origin is the very important discovery made at Kalakh, on the right bank of the Tigris in southern Mesopotamia, by an English archeological expedition. This polychrome plaque from a casket [figure 16] displays a very different style from that of the Egyptian objects; the whole plaque is covered, as in marquetry or stained glass, with interlaced lines and volumes representing a thicket of plants surrounding the protagonists of the drama – a lion attacking a Negro. This scene was doubtlessly intended as a form of defence, by suggesting the fate of anyone who should appropriate the contents of the casket covered by the plaque.

When we come to the Greeks, it is still the most ancient works that are the finest, and the majority are religious. One of the best known pieces is in the museum at Candia, the

5 A late Roman pyx from Sens Cathedral, typical of those found in church treasures. They played an important part in transmitting pagan themes to Romanesque art

6 This plaque from the right-hand side of a Roman diptych in the Hellenistic style (*c* 400 AD) refers to a marriage between two Roman families

famous acrobat who seems to be descending from the sky like an arrow to take part in a sacred bull-fight. The art of grouping sculptural figures in some common activity was already understood in Crete and at Mycenae. Sculptured figures comparable to those from Crete have also been found in Cyprus [figure 17]. We know from ancient authors of the chryselephantine sculpture of the classical Greeks: colossal figures in which the visible flesh-parts were carved in ivory and the draperies made from plates of gold inset with precious stones or glass on wooden frames, with some of the attributes in bronze. There were many examples of this technique in classical times, some of the best known being Pheidias' Pallas Athene at Athens and Zeus at Olympia and Polycleitus' Hera at Argos; if we can trust the ancient writers, the aesthetic effect was magnificent.

There has been much speculation as to how ivory was made to cover the very large surfaces, and it was long believed that the Greeks must have had some special technique for softening it and flattening it out. However, all the suggested recipes have failed, and it seems probable that the large expanses were made from small pieces dowelled together, as in the earlier Greek marble sculptures. The few pieces of chryselephantine sculpture which were found at Delphi were lifesize, small enough for the head to have been carved from a single piece. Given the mastery of the Greeks in marble, the importance of ivory carving was not as great in the classical period as in the preceding periods, and, although in the Middle Ages classical antiquity retained considerable authority, it was the style of earlier works that was to be revived at the time of the invasion of eastern fashions.

There are two kinds of object which show the persistence of classical styles and, at the same time, the prevalence of small reliefs and the miniature style. They were to continue throughout the Middle Ages, and even longer. First there was the pyx, a circular jewel box used by Roman women, later sometimes conserved in church treasuries and used for the reservation of the Sacrament. Decorated with hunting scenes, the pyx illustrated here [figure 5] shows us the delicate modelling, suggestive of volume in spite of its shallowness, which characterized these objects. Later on they were to be engraved with Christian subjects; for instance, we see Christ surrounded by the apostles on the Syrian-style pyx in Berlin.

The other important form was the diptych [figures 6 and 7]. These double plaques, joined together and with their inner faces covered with wax, served as writing tablets [figure 60]. Some of the earlier examples are known as 'consular diptychs', since it was customary, between 400 and 540 AD, for them to be presented to the Emperor by consuls on the occasion of their investiture. When these diptychs became part of a church treasury, the names of saints, benefactors, or bishops were substituted for those of the consuls. The outside is generally decorated with scenes from circus games given to celebrate triumphs, or later with the images of saints (the ivory book in Rouen Cathedral) or of angels (British Museum).

More important diptychs with five compartments, known as 'imperial diptychs' (the finest, called the 'Barberini ivory' in the Louvre, shows the Emperor defeating his enemies) were the inspiration for designs on covers for the Gospels, the figures of victory becoming angels. Even larger objects were simply composed of plaques of the same description. At Alexandria and Constantinople (Byzantium), imperial iconography was taken over in Christian art; this can be seen in the episcopal throne at Ravenna [figure 8], a masterpiece of early Christian ivory carving, possibly of Byzantine origin, on which we see figures of the saints associated with scenes from the life of Joseph, friezes of animals, etc.

The contribution of classical antiquity was a fundamental one; it was to be enriched and completed in the Carolingian and Romanesque epochs, and must not be confused with the

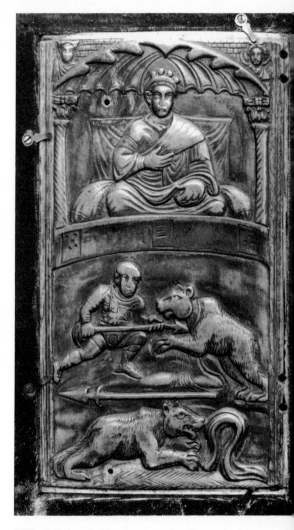

7 The left-hand side of a Consular Diptych, showing the holes used for the cords which fastened the two sides together

8 The splendid Byzantine throne of Bishop Maximian (6th century) shows how St John the Baptist and the Evangelists inherited the framework of arches, columns and baldachini which once surrounded emperors

very important influence of Constantinople in creating the formulae used in the Middle Ages and transmitting antique themes. In imitation of the miniatures on manuscripts, the ivory plaques on bookcovers [figure 1] were crowded with scenes illustrating Holy Writ. The crucifixion was the central theme, but allegories of early origin were associated with it, involving Earth, Ocean, the cities of Rome and Jerusalem, the ancient and the new Alliances and the future of the church (represented by the evangelists and their animal symbols), so that the whole of space and time were associated with the supreme sacrifice. It would be difficult to imagine so noble a conception expressed in a more restricted space.

The finest Carolingian works are Germanic in origin, in the style known as Ottonian. The antique tradition is especially reflected in them, following the Byzantine influence. The Tournus flabellum, a liturgical fan modelled on the fly-whisks of eastern potentates, consists of a wheel supported on a long handle decorated with superimposed designs; attached to it is a box with scenes inspired by Virgil's eclogues.

The triptych form, which was to be in great favour throughout the Gothic period, was of Byzantine origin. The finest, the Harbaville triptych [figure 9], is in the Louvre, and one may admire the religious iconography and the rich decoration of the outsides of the panels, representing cypress trees bowing before the triumphant cross. But the most attractive form found in Byzantine art is that of the rectangular secular caskets [figure 10], common from ancient times and later imitated by Gothic artists and found in great numbers among church treasuries. The 'Veroli casket', in the Victoria and Albert Museum, is an example from the cathedral at Veroli. Circus games, divinities or ancient heroes decorate these caskets, and the plaques are joined together with simple wooden tenons. Although these were everyday objects, their elegance charms us.

Byzantine influence predominated in the Western cradle

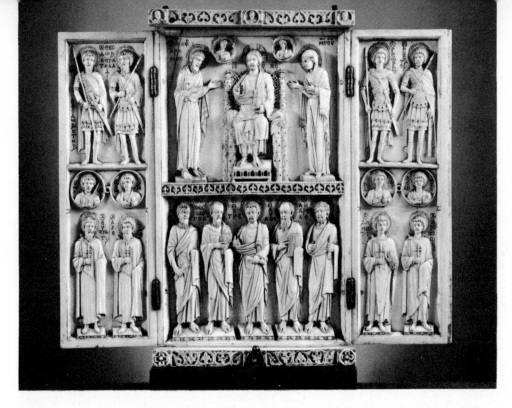

9 An open triptych with all its faces ornamented. Christ has taken the place once occupied by the Emperor between the sun and moon (Constantinople, late 10th century)

of Romanesque art, especially after the iconoclasm. On the Germanic-Romanesque plaque illustrated in figure 12 the half-length angels on the arms of the cross and the holy women visiting Christ's tomb are entirely Byzantine in feeling. Although it has obviously been influenced by northern artists and English miniaturists, the famous English bone plaque of the *Adoration of the Magi* in the Victoria and Albert Museum also manifests a lively Byzantine influence, shown in the unequal size and conventional treatment of the figures.

However, Romanesque art cannot be reduced to terms of pure imitation of the Byzantine. This is proved by the episcopal croziers. One cannot conceive of greater elegance and sobriety of line than is displayed by the Italian crozier illustrated here [figure 13] ending in a dragon's head, according to the current formula.

10 An exquisite secular Byzantine casket of the 11th century decorated with themes from classical antiquity: Orpheus, the Sibyl, cupids

Another more archaic form, giving scope for the richly fantastic animal and vegetable decoration of Romanesque art, is that of the tau, an ivory staff, also designed for a bishop's use but topped by a crutch-like bar. On the Rouen tau we see a wolf threatening its victim caught in a tangle of interlace. It does not seem that such images could be purely decorative. Dragons from hell or hunting scenes express the idea that the world is full of problems and conflicts, and that the bishop's mission is to resolve them [figure 14].

Byzantine influence can be seen in a class of secular ivory objects, the hunting-horns, or oliphants, of which a large number have survived. This class has always presented considerable problems of attribution, the difficulty being to distinguish those which are actually of eastern workmanship

11 Statuette of a Thinite
king found at Abydos.
He is wearing the crown
of Upper Egypt and the
cloak of the Sed Festival,
but has lost his legs,
sceptre, and flagellum
(Egyptian, 4th millennium)

12 A 10th-century German Crucifixion showing strong Byzantine influence

from western examples showing a strong eastern influence. Some of the surviving pieces in this class are actually of Byzantine workmanship, many having been preserved as reliquaries in western church treasuries, into which they found their way after the sack of Constantinople by the Crusaders in 1204.

The eleventh-century hunting-horn in figure 15 shows the difficulties involved. The scheme of Christ in glory in a nimbus supported by flying angels above an arch in which the Virgin prays, the successive bands of formal ornament, and in particular the treatment of the birds and animals contained in two of the surrounding bands would all suggest a Coptic Egyptian or perhaps even a Syrian origin. In fact, this horn is probably Germanic work, and the characteristic northern interlace which appears in two of the bands suggests this. In the oliphant from the museum at Angers [figure 18] the animals — lions and camels — would at first suggest an oriental origin, but the probability is that this piece again is western. This is suggested by the fluidity of modelling of the figures; it probably dates from a little later, the twelfth century. Many of the horns of this period were enriched with decoration in enamel or with silver rings, and we read of their magnificence in such works as the *Lay of the Horn*. In *Huon de Bordeaux* (late twelfth century) we are told that the horn belonging to the dwarf Oberon was decorated with pendants made of gold and pearls.

A remarkable instance of the use of ivory in religious works in the Romanesque period is seen in the splendid gilt bronze and enamel reliquaries from Cologne [figure 20], which follow the central dome plan of a Byzantine church. The small statues of apostles and large carved plaques fixed under the arcades of these extraordinary objects are made of ivory. But it is above all in the Gothic ivories of the thirteenth century, which to some extent reflect the full-sized sculpture of the time, that one can see a religious art that had achieved perfect equilibrium and serenity, reminiscent

18

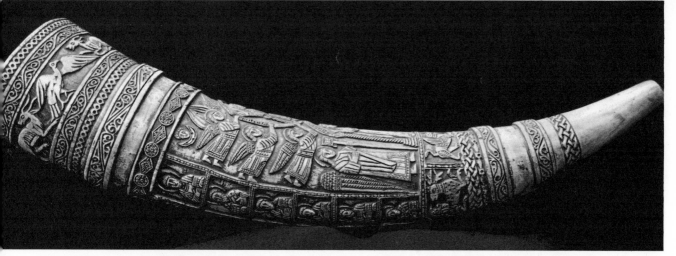

of the beauty of Greek marbles. It is as if the universal glorification of the Virgin, visible in monuments of widely different sorts and in the consecration of cathedrals to the Mother of God, were in some way the purified and transcendent outcome of the cult of Venus and other great goddesses.

In this connection, the most remarkable group is the polychrome *Coronation of the Virgin* [figure 19] in the Louvre. The folds, the outlines of the figures, the angels' smiles belong to stone statuary, but at the same time one is aware of a richness (to become more marked later on) and a fine

13 *(top left)* Italian crozier of the Romanesque period. The figure three (dragon's horns and point of the gonfalon) signifies that Christ's agony lasted for three days

14 *(top right)* The 'Alcester Tau', an Anglo-Norman crozier (early 11th century) showing both Coptic and Celtic influences

15 *(above)* An 11th-century German oliphant revealing a marked oriental influence in both theme and treatment

17 *(above)* The animated hunting scene on this casket from Enkomi, Cyprus (14th century BC) demonstrates the strength of Egyptian influence in Cyprus

16 *(opposite)* An Assyrian plaque displaying a new technique of semi-relief as well as a great mastery of polychromy and inlay (Nimrud Kalakh, 8th century BC)

finish, which make it impossible to consider such ivories simply as great sculpture in reduced form. Another masterpiece of Gothic ivory carving, the diptych supposed to have come from the cathedral at Soissons [figure 22], whereon the cycle of the Passion is unrolled, proves that Christ had not been forgotten; although the figures are so small and the gabled architectural background so important, the scenes follow one another with perfect lucidity.

While we have a number of images of Virgin and Child, Crucifixions from this period are rare. The Christ from the Abbey of Herlufsholm in Denmark [figure 23] is therefore all the more precious. In contrast to the dramatic approach of the latter part of the Middle Ages, we see here a classical restraint, a refusal to let the harmony of line be sacrificed to the suffering portrayed; the elegance of the drapery is unequalled and might have come from Villard de Honnecourt's sketch-book.

We have met with no shortage of masterpieces in this rapid sketch of the origins of ivory carving, and many others could have been mentioned. Why, then, is it necessary to lay even more stress on the ensuing period: the end of the Middle Ages, the Renaissance, and the age of baroque? Because, despite the excellence of the ivories belonging to the period we have just been considering, and the added value they gain from the fact that other works of the time have vanished, those from the fourteenth century onwards are more remarkable still. Up to this point the Middle Ages had mainly produced religious objects: flabella (fans), liturgical buckets (situlae), diptychs, altar fronts, or bookcovers, none of which could be freely designed by their creators, who had to submit to the rules of iconography. Religious objects continued to be made — diptychs, triptychs, polyptychs, retables, private altars, paxes, memento mori or rosary beads — but they were likely to be ordered for individual use, and thus more susceptible to fantasy and variation.

Secular artifacts also multiplied, such as jewel-boxes,

18 This hunting horn shows that western artists had assimilated oriental influences by the 12th century

mirror-cases, stick-handles, saddles, knives, *gravoirs*, combs, belt-buckles, pieces and dice for various games, chess, backgammon, etc. During the sixteenth, seventeenth, and eighteenth centuries, tobacco-graters and priming-flasks were made; in the seventeenth and eighteenth centuries, tankards, salt-cellars, Germanic goblets, vases, scent-bottles, huntingflasks, game-dishes, shuttles, tobacco-jars, knife-handles, etc. Even slippers or shoes for skating were made of ivory! These objects may well have enhanced the personal prestige of their owners, but they did the same for their makers, although signatures only began to appear during the baroque age.

Romanesque art, although dominated by Germany, had become an art of the whole of Europe. In the early Gothic

19 *The Coronation of the Virgin*, a Gothic group of consummate artistry and exquisite delicacy, exemplifying the cult of the Virgin at its height

23

20 The 'Eltenberg Reliquary', the most famous of the Cologne
reliquaries. These objects, which reveal Byzantine influence, represent
the 'divine city' of the Apocalypse

21 In many of the polyptychs and triptychs of this sort, the gestures of
the figures in the four scenes on the panels have deep symbolical
significance

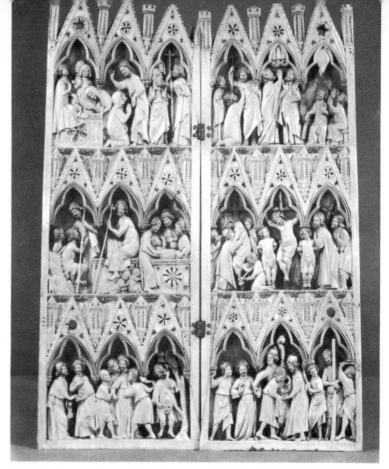

22 A diptych, said to have come from Soissons Cathedral, which belongs to one of the earliest and most important groups of French Gothic ivory carvings

period, France alone reigned supreme, but ivory carving was from that time onwards to be a European art. From the fourteenth century onwards the supremacy of France began to decline, and other national styles developed, particularly those of England and Italy. Later on, during the age of baroque, the Flemish, Spanish, and Italian styles became more defined, in spite of a renewal of German influence.

The diversification of styles was also due to the fact that from this date artists began attempting to reproduce in ivory everything that had originally been made in other materials. The small English diptychs reflect contemporary architecture even more faithfully than do those of the true Gothic period. In England and in Germany, alabaster bas-reliefs were recreated in ivory. French and German retables might equally well be made of precious metals or ivory. In Flanders paxes sometimes copied wood-engravings, statuettes or groups from wood-carvings. This trend was to reach its peak in the baroque period, when bas-reliefs on plaques, goblets, vases, and salt-cellars often reflected the most ambitious ventures of contemporary sculpture or painting, even copying Michelangelo's sculptures or Rubens' paintings!

While describing the tendency of European carvers to multiply the possible uses to which ivory could be put, we must not neglect the Gothic trends persisting through the fourteenth and fifteenth centuries and even later; we shall here be concerned with small objects like knife-handles, powder-flasks and graters. Indeed, workers in ivory had to conform to such narrow limitations that only Gothic art (with its inheritance from the past) could keep strictly to them, and the workmanship of these small objects carried on the Gothic tradition in more than one respect.

What, then, is ivory? From where does it come? What were the limitations it imposed? At the present moment, when we possess so many materials capable of producing similar effects, it is difficult to imagine the prestige ivory enjoyed from antiquity until the Middle Ages, or even the eighteenth century. In medieval times it was reputed to have come from the mysterious country of the Queen of Sheba. People also believed that its origin was the horn of the unicorn, symbol of virginity (the horn-like tooth of the narwhal was commonly believed to be a unicorn's horn), and this is undoubtedly the reason that so many religious objects made of ivory were consecrated to the Virgin. Dante, however, makes ivory symbolical of falsehood. The prestige of ivory is also connected with the legend of Roland and his famous oliphant, and with the fact that it was principally through these small ivory objects that the great art of antiquity was revealed to the people of the Middle Ages.

The prestige of ivory can also be explained by the special

23 In this sublime Crucifixion, the artist has clearly been inspired by wood-carvings and Romanesque figures of Christ

24 A 14th-century French mirror-case; the workmanship is extremely delicate and the symbolic theme of a man with crossed legs can be seen

25 A 15th-century casket from northern Italy or Flanders decorated with courtly scenes

26 A Siculo-Arabic box (14th century); next to the man on a dromedary is the western symbol of an eagle

29

qualities of the material, to which no-one can remain indifferent. Ivory absorbs and reflects light, and is enriched by it. Its high cost is explained by its rarity, and the distance from which it comes, varying for place and period. In the beginning, as we have seen, mammoth tusks were used, as well as elephant tusks and antlers of deer or chamois. From 3000 BC the Egyptians used elephant tusks from the Sudan or hippopotamus teeth from the Nile. The Phoenicians kept a large herd of elephants in Syria; it was decimated by the Assyrians in the eighth century BC, a fact which explains their important output of works of art in ivory, and its later decline. Rome and Byzantium used tusks of elephants from India and Egypt and of walrus imported by Viking traders. The northern countries, particularly England, constantly used walrus ivory, and the Arabs made handles for their daggers and sabres from it.

In the Middle Ages ivory from West Africa was most commonly used, shipped from the Ethiopian port of Zeyla and from Aden, as well as Alexandria and Acre, and through Famagusta. On the whole, India provided less ivory than Africa because it was burnt there in honour of their gods, and the elephant was spared as a sacred animal. When ivory became the fashion later on in Flanders and Germany, it was because it arrived in abundant quantity at the great North Sea ports during the seventeenth century, and the sailors from Dieppe used to go in search of *morphi* on their expeditions to West Africa.

Ivory is, for the most part, easy to work, but varies according to its provenance. There are, in fact, different sorts of ivory; in comparison with the best ivory from elephants, hippopotami, narwhals, mammoths, and walrus, that from whale-bone is less valuable and easily becomes rubbed. Ivory from elephant or walrus tusks is in a category of its own. Ivory is a living substance which improves and hardens with age. Siamese ivory turns yellow, whereas ivory from West Africa becomes whiter; after a certain time veins appear in it and broaden till the ivory seems to be milky white all over. Ivory from Ceylon turns a pale pink.

Elephant ivory is composed of lozenge-shaped fibres arranged concentrically. Since all the tusks used for ivory are hollow and curved, the tusks of the African elephant, being the longest, are the most highly prized: they may measure up to ten feet. They are also the straightest, while those of the mammoth are the most curved. Even plaques cut from the middle and straightest part of a tusk cannot be more than six to eight inches wide.

The material imposes its own restrictions. Given the limited dimensions of the plaques, a technique based on the similar art of miniature has to be adopted. The patient work of the old *pigniers*, or comb-makers, cutting away flake after flake and respecting the grain of the ivory, set off its texture better than did the use of the lathe which appeared during the Renaissance. In the case of large pieces made of several plaques, it was hardly possible to avoid the join being visible, however discreetly. Various tools were needed: a saw to cut the plaques, a probe to hollow out the cavity in the tusk, files to smooth the surface, chisel and mallet for carving, burins and scrapers to mould the forms. And the ivory had to be kept wet all the time or else it would change colour.

Gothic ivories followed traditional pictorial techniques. One may wonder why secular ivories dating from the end of the Middle Ages, such as the cover of a set of writing-tablets representing the *Coronation of a Lady* [figure 28], a secularized version of the *Coronation of the Virgin*, should depict the lovers wearing stylized garments like those of religious personages, instead of the complicated fashions of the day. It is because these clothes more clearly reveal essential gestures, such as the arm of the woman pointing to her betrothed. The gestures are exaggerated, and so is the size of the important parts of the body; the heads, for instance, are always large in proportion to the rest so as to set off their luminous whiteness.

28 A French writing tablet of the 14th century showing the *Coronation of a Lady*

27 (*opposite*) The Virgin of the Sainte Chapelle, once decorated with jewels and gilding, is a perfect example of the transition from Gothic classicism to the affected style of the 14th century

This deliberate simplification, which does not exclude depth of thought or subtle implications, is very different from the perhaps excessive complexity of the plaques of the baroque epoch, such as Elhafen's *Rape of the Sabines* [figure 30]. Here all the new techniques of the Renaissance are used with undeniable vigour: *sfumato* (or *chiaroscuro*), perspective, movement, anatomy, treatment skilfully varied for flesh, clothes or foliage. But the multiplication of planes, fragmentation of the ivory, and careful shading have an effect very different from that produced in stone or bronze; they result in an all-over greyness, and the landscapes detract from the effectiveness of the whole.

Some of the most successful plaques, the most classical in

29 *(opposite)* The Salting Diptych; the frontal view lends majesty to the figures of Christ and the Virgin

30 A plaque by the German carver Elhafen, which shows the influence of Italian baroque sculpture

style since Egypt, present the figures against a plain background. However, the baroque bas-reliefs will be thought superior to Simon Troger's ambitious sculptured group [figure 31] of the same date, in which wood and ivory are combined in one vast composition, *The Judgement of Solomon*. The materials are sandwiched together in a rather charmless way, in spite of the quality of the sculpture and its freedom of movement. In general the vast ambitions of the Renaissance and the baroque age found only limited scope in the domain of ivory carving, and their large subjects were less successful than the smaller, utilitarian objects in which they expressed themselves more happily and produced masterpieces equal to those of the end of the Middle Ages.

In spite of the unusual fascination of its whiteness, ivory has been pigmented in every epoch. It is not known exactly how the Egyptians coloured their ivories, but they probably soaked them in baths of mineral salts: red, yellow, brown, green or black malachite. The Phoenicians and Mesopotamians not only coloured ivory but encrusted the reliefs with gold and lapislazuli. The most important pieces from the Middle Ages — Virgins in glory, ceremonial saddles, chessboards, caskets, etc — combined ivory with cabochons, precious stones, gilt, and enamel. Reminiscent of the famous golden Virgin of Amiens, the very beautiful Virgin and Child occupying the centre of a polyptych [figure 21] belongs to the best Gothic period, when serene nobility was not compromised by affectation or mannerism; the Child is large and solemn, the Virgin's body scarcely twisted, the folds logical. Discreet polychromy accentuates the lines; the clothes are edged with embroidery, the hair gilt, the flesh pink.

This Virgin closely resembles one that is described as 'of the Sainte Chapelle' [figure 27]. But we know from an inventory that Charles V loaded her with jewels, gilt, and coats of arms, which have since disappeared. There was a silver-gilt escutcheon with the arms of France in enamel, supported by five little lions; the Child wore an agate cameo, the Virgin a gold crown, pearls and diamonds. One is reminded of the chryselephantine statues.

Polychromy also occured in Byzantine art, with red inscriptions and gilded figures. During the seventeenth and eighteenth centuries figures representing, paradoxically it seems, beggars and the minor trades by Krüger and Köhler in Germany and some artists in other parts of Europe [figure 132] were placed on silver-gilt pedestals and were sometimes themselves pigmented. Here we can see a new stage in the secularization of an art that had been hieratic at its outset, the counterpart of the realistic tavern and genre scenes of Caravaggio and the Dutch school.

What particularly interests us about the fourteenth and fifteenth centuries is that they show us the first stage of this secularization: the transition from a religious art to an art of the court and nobility, or even of the bourgeoisie in the case of small utilitarian objects, at least in France. The following three centuries were to see this process of secularization spread all over Europe. In Italian Renaissance ivories the religious retained as much emphasis as the purely plastic. The German output of the seventeenth century represented an art that was pre-eminently of the court, and blossomed in a variety of genres. In eighteenth-century France, ivory carving became predominantly the province of the artisan.

Ivory carving remains an art, even if it is a minor one, and the material deserves to be considered in its own right. However, limitations of space forbid dealing with cases where it is subordinated to another material, as in the wood inlaid with ivory often used in Egypt for furniture, and during the Renaissance and the seventeenth century, in Italy and France as well as in Spain, for caskets. Many ivory objects, such as cobblers' measures, spindles, hourglasses, or busks for women's stays, are of little artistic value. In Holland, also, a great number of absurd or even obscene little figures, buffoons, swashbucklers, etc were made, which are not worth our notice.

31 The German carver Troger (1693/4—1769) executed this important group in a somewhat charmless combination of wood and ivory

36

# CHAPTER TWO

# The Gothic Tradition

IT MAY BE WONDERED why such a large amount of space has been devoted in this study to the works of the Middle Ages. The reason for this emphasis is that the earlier works are often the most beautiful (partly because of the formal limitations restricting them); afterwards the same forms were repeated indefinitely. Such was the case with diptychs; only the decorative scheme changed with the passage of time. There are, of course, noticeable differences between an ivory from the beginning of the fourteenth century and one from the end of the fifteenth, although not always to the advantage of the latter. But within the given form there are only very small stylistic variations by which to date such objects as mirror-cases or caskets, and that with a certain margin of error.

Throughout this period France dominated the scene, although precariously in the fifteenth century, for ivory carving seems to have become an international art from the end of the fourteenth century. Raymond Koechlin's important work, *French Gothic Ivories* (1924), has emphasized French supremacy. We have documentary proof of the intense activity of the guild of ivory workers in Paris, and we learn from Etienne Boileau's *Book of Trades* that in 1250 ivory was among the materials used by 'carvers and makers of images and crucifixes'. Carvers of the images of saints were in a special category, along with makers of religious objects, statuettes, plaquettes, tabernacles, and altar-pieces.

33 French crozier in the classical style

32 (*opposite*) Scenes from the Childhood of Christ; the left-hand panel of a diptych 'decorated with roses' (French, early 14th century)

34 and 35 The same conception of the Trinity can be seen in these ivory (*above*) and alabaster (*opposite*) groups. The latter is colder and more vertical, whereas the former has a more fluid line, following the shape of the material

There were other categories also: cutlers, *pigniers* (makers of combs and mirror-cases), makers of handles, chess-boards, dice, and rosaries. Other writers tell us about Parisian ivory carvers who worked for various noble houses, especially in Burgundy during the reign of Philippe VI. Jean le Braellier, goldsmith and ivory worker employed by Mahaut d'Artois, worked at the court of Hesdin and at Dijon for Bonne de Bourbon; Jean le Couilly for Monseigneur the Duc de Bourbon (from 1355 to 1357) and Bertrand 'l'échéqueur' for Robert d'Artois.

We cannot accept the hypotheses of D. D. Egbert (*North Italian Gothic Ivories in the Museo Cristiano of the Vatican Library*, 1929) and of C. R. Morey (*Italian Gothic Ivories in Medieval Studies in memory of Kingsley Porter*), who tried to prove the existence of an Italian workshop earlier than, and quite distinct from, that of the Embriachi, producing work very different from the French. On the other hand, ivories were being made in England, and their special characteristics must be defined. Although of as high quality as the French ivories, they were less abundant, and Miss M. H. Longhurst (*English Ivories*) has perhaps given England rather too much credit.

The most serious attack against Koechlin's theory comes from Hazeloff (*Repertorium für Kunstwissenschaft*, 1926), who holds that ivory carving was, like miniature-painting, preponderantly a French art, but practised in many other European countries simultaneously. However, there has been much more difficulty in identifying rival workshops with any degree of certainty in the case of ivories than in the case of miniatures, although a very strong case has been put for the existence of an important Rhenish school at Cologne working in a style fairly similar to the French during the first half of the fourteenth century, and many quite important pieces which Koechlin considered to be French have more recently been re-attributed to Cologne by some authorities.

Although France's supremacy undeniably continued during the fourteenth century, it had already been breached at the end of it by the rivalry of the Embriachi, especially in the domain of secular artifacts, and during the fifteenth century ivory carving became (as it has remained ever since) a fully international art. Clear proof of the birth of this internationalism is to be seen in some retables (Poissy), groups (the Langres Annunciation), polychrome secular caskets, and paxes. Most of these works must be attributed to Flemish or northern French workshops or to the numerous Italians working in those regions at the time. Only a few saddles, knife-handles, or other utilitarian objects like belt-buckles have come down to us, but those that we possess seem to prove that German and Italian workshops existed of which we have now lost track. French ivory workers shone particularly in religious art, and the Scandinavian countries must have gone on making chessmen from walrus ivory, in imitation of early models seen in the south.

Let us first examine some religious works revealing France's supremacy, together with some secular artifacts, caskets, and mirror-cases, also of the highest quality. The secular ivories are more original, but as with the religious works, the concentration and depth of the ideas they contain relate them to cathedral statuary.

We must return to the theme of Virgin and Child (of which we have already given a beautiful example in polychrome), for most of the religious objects can be grouped around this central subject. As well as standing Virgins, many seated Virgins were made, a return to the Romanesque tradition. The infant Christ became more realistic, and was dressed in a shift. The once straight, regular folds of the Virgin's robe were now more complicated, with scroll-like convolutions. The Virgin's figure was at first bent sideways, then elongated, then compact.

The figures of the Virgin and Child of the fourteenth century had become markedly more human since the time of

36 The theme of the 'Virgin and Child' becomes a theme of 'Maternity' in the 14th century, as seen in this French group

37 *(opposite)* This group from a retable gives an impression of monumental splendour in spite of the shallowness of the relief

the haughty Virgin of the Sainte Chapelle. In early examples she was still majestic and her dress hung in regular folds; the figures were supported on a polygonal base as before. The Child made awkward, unexpected gestures; sometimes his hand rested on the clasp of the Virgin's robe. Other groups show an even more unusual innovation; the Virgin is giving her breast to the Child on her lap. The final stage of this evolution can be seen in one of the most lively groups of the latter half of the fourteenth century [figure 36]; the late date is indicated by the riotous folds, the Virgin's long torso, and the way the Child flings himself upon her, while she draws back.

Very different is the graceful, refined Virgin attributed with good reason to Giovanni Pisano. *The Langres Annunciation*, an early fifteenth century polychrome group, displays a new picturesque approach; the quality of the work and the rich colouring redeem the element of caricature in the gestures and in the profiles with their turned-up noses. Finally, during the Renaissance, figures of the Virgin suffered a radical change. The naked Child became a cherub, the Virgin a great lady in an ample robe with soft folds. She was supported on a square pedestal decorated with Renaissance grotesques. An example is the Virgin and Child in the Louvre, formerly in the Davillier Collection. This is almost certainly Spanish, but the style could equally be Italian or Flemish. It illustrates the way a new international style had supplanted Gothic.

Some objects, such as triptychs, retables, and polyptychs disappeared with the Middle Ages. In the baroque period the groups decorating altars were to develop a very different style. Before they started to create the vast retables for churches, of which only fragments survive [figure 37], the ivory carvers had fashioned a great number of triptychs and polyptychs. As in Byzantine triptychs, the folding panels were attached to a central one, but they were now crowned with triangular gables. These were for private altars, which could easily be opened out for evening or morning prayers or during family devotions. They would be kept in the alcove by the bed behind a praying-stool, but the chapel was close to the bedrooms in the houses of middle-class families and the nobility alike. The number of panels was a sign of wealth. These portable altars could be taken on a journey; they were shut up in wooden chests made of stamped leather resting on trestles. They remained in favour until enamels and paintings took their place.

The Virgin and Child were carved in the round in the centre of most of the triptychs and polyptychs, and the treatment of this group makes it possible to date the work. There is also one very curious example showing the close relationship between the two forms, groups and retables. The Virgin of Boubon opens herself to reveal three panels of a triptych on which the cycle of the Passion is unrolled.

As a general rule we find arranged around the central Virgin and Child the cycle of the Nativity or Childhood of Christ in four scenes: the Visitation and Annunciation (combined), the Nativity (Joseph is usually presenting the Child to the Virgin), the Presentation in the Temple (this scene is complementary; the Virgin presents the Child to the High Priest), and lastly the Adoration of the Magi (they are manifestly adoring the infant Christ held in the arms of the central Virgin). On the polyptychs the scenes are no more numerous; it is merely that the figures are larger and occupy four panels instead of two, as in the triptychs [figure 21]. Sometimes scenes from the Passion will occupy a third register.

The apparent monotony of the four scenes, always in the same position on either side of the Virgin, is not fortuitous but of profound significance. We know what a deep meaning was given to the theme of the tetramorph, or the four evangelical beasts, in the art and dogma of the Middle Ages; the Angel, Ox, Lion, and Eagle appeared in a vision to Ezekiel and Saint John. They were interpreted not only as the four

42

apostles themselves (Matthew, Luke, Mark, and John), but also as stages in the life of Christ (Incarnation, Death or Sacrifice, Resurrection, Ascension); or lastly, as the virtues of a Christian, desirous of imitating his Master. The four scenes taken from Christ's childhood have an identical significance and are placed in the same order around the central Virgin as the animals. The Visitation is equated with the Incarnation and Matthew, at the top on the left; the Nativity with the Ascension and the Eagle, at the top on the right; the Presentation with the Ox (Christ being offered to the Priest at the altar, as if sacrificing himself in advance), below on the right; while the Magi receiving the good news represent the Resurrection, below on the left.

There are few triptychs illustrating the life of Christ which do not express some such profound allegory as the above. On the other hand, when the Virgin and Child do not figure on the central panel, one often finds a complete cycle consecrated to the Virgin on all three registers carried across the three panels [figure 39]. The Childhood of Christ appears below, so that as before the emphasis is on the role of the Mother; the death of the Virgin occupies the second register, following Byzantine and apocryphal iconography, according to which the apostles surround her death-bed, and Christ receives her soul; finally in the third register, the Coronation of the Virgin.

French pieces are as deeply edifying as cathedral sculpture, but Italian retables and triptychs [figure 38], on the other hand, aim only at pleasing. Furthermore, the carving of Italian pieces is of inferior quality because the material employed is bone; the sumptuosity of these objects is in their frames, often made of the skilful marquetry known as *alla certosina*, making use of Greek or other antique motifs. The figures are graceful, and no longer express any deep dogmatic intention. Instead they tell a story, sometimes a very complex one, with the Crucifixion as the central theme.

We see in all these characteristics the dawn of the Re-

39 A triptych devoted entirely to the Virgin. From the bottom upwards: the Childhood of Christ, the Death of the Virgin, the Coronation

38 (*opposite*) Italian retable of the Embriachi school showing scenes from the Passion and the Nativity with figures of Saints

naissance. Already in the Romanesque period the altar frontal at Palermo was planned on a grand scale. In order to combine an almost unlimited number of scenes, Italian retables are sometimes very large. The Poissy retable (as it is called) in the Louvre, attributed to Benedetto da Majano, contains sixty-three bas-reliefs, and describes the lives of John the Baptist and Saint John the Evangelist as well as Christ's. The retable in the monastery at Pavia is even more impressive. Another style was soon to appear in northern France and Flanders. Again the Virgin and Child occupied the middle, but the general effect was much more massive than that of Gothic retables, and they were overloaded with gilding, pigmentation, and marquetry, as in the altar at Bruges: a manifestation of the decadence of a style.

The same contrast between French and Italian works is to be seen in the more interesting secular artifacts, that is to say, caskets and mirror-cases. On one side we have a scholarly art with systematic iconography, closely related to religious art; on the other, a narrative style with emphasis on the decorative aspect.

Mirror-cases were made of two circular plaques joined either by a cord passing through a hole or else by a metal

40 and 41 The smaller side *(left)* and cover *(right)* of a late 14th-century casket showing the combination of secular scenes (the story of Perceval) with religious ones (the four saints)

joint. Inside them was a metal disc serving as a mirror, and both outer surfaces were decorated. As for the caskets, they were oblong after Byzantine models, and made of five pieces of ivory joined together with iron pins; the lid was opened by a metal handle. These caskets could be locked, and were used for jewels, articles of toilet, scents, etc.

The subjects ornamenting mirror-cases and caskets are neither particularly edifying nor very varied; most often we are shown pairs of lovers pierced by the arrows of the God of Love, riding in the forest, playing chess, crowning one another [figure 28], dancing the 'carole', etc. A casket plaque, *The Stag-hunt* [figure 42], illustrates an unusual theme from tales of chivalry; a mirror-case in the Liverpool museum, *The Abduction of a Lady*, is said to represent Queen Guinevere, and another in the Museo Civico at Bologna, *Gawain on the Perilous Bed*, is in the same vein. Koechlin distinguishes several sorts of subject to be found on caskets: those concerned with gallantry, such as we have been describing, romantic subjects, and lastly, composite subjects, in which both themes are combined. We sometimes

42 The late date of this 'composite' plaque of a casket is revealed by the elaborate carving and graduated planes. The stag-hunting episode comes from romances of chivalry

45

43 and 44 Two sides of a 'composite' casket. Short side: Galahad and the Guardian of the Castle; long side: the Lay of Aristotle, and the Fountain of Youth

find religious subjects, but generally late in our period [figures 40 and 41].

However, the repetition of the same themes and gestures must not blind us to the extraordinarily condensed symbolism, for the rites of courtly love are transposed versions of religious rites as can clearly be seen in works recently attributed to Germany. We have already remarked that the pairs of lovers wore clothes more suitable to religious figures; in the same way the architectural settings of gables and columns in the mirror-cases are similar to those in religious ivories.

Two mirror-cases in London (attributed by some authorities to Cologne), illustrating The Attack on the Castle of Love [figure 48], represent square castles in the style of the Holy City of the Apocalypse or the Castle of the Grail; they have three storeys and one of them even has a three-fold balustrade (three is the figure symbolizing love). The tournament in the foreground is a ritual by means of which the victor can ascend and attack the castle, which is defended from the balcony by 'virgins' with roses (*The Romaunt of the Rose*). On one of these cases, the God of Love is seen with two pairs of wings like a cherub. A mirror-case from the Cluny museum [figure 45] presents an esoteric image: man, the Master, stands with his feet on a lion, being crowned by an angel, and dominates the submissive woman whose feet are on a dragon. On the right, the three ages of man. A recurrent motif is a pair of crossed legs [figure 24]; these, among other symbolic meanings (and symbols always have many meanings), indicate the strict discipline to which man must submit, and the necessity of keeping instinct in check. We know what innumerable obstacles the heroes of romance had to overcome before they reached the *'princesse lointaine'*.

The greatest number of symbolic meanings is combined in the 'composite' caskets, as they are called, relatively few in number, in which broadly similar series of tests are arranged according to a regular scheme. Dangers, love-tests, exaltation of virginity through the fable of the unicorn, are depicted on the sides. The Attack on the Castle of Love is displayed on the lid [figure 46]; the four scenes surrounding the tournament, and particularly the ascent (Ascension) in the top at the right, refer to the idea of the four animals within the four tasks that the knight has to perform, as in the scenes surrounding the Virgin in polyptychs. On one side [figure 44] we have Aristotle teaching Alexander and the Disgrace of Aristotle (Aristotle ridden by the courtesan Campaspe under the mocking eyes of Alexander) signifying the dangers of senile love, and episodes showing rejuvenation in the Fountain of Youth. On one end [figure 43], Galahad

45 A French mirror-case full of symbols, particularly the position of the lady's two feet on the two-legged dragon (the figure four represents Woman)

46 The theme of the 'Attack on the Castle' is repeated everywhere on the lids of 'composite' caskets

47

47 As in ivories, secular and religious themes (the 'Bridge of Swords' and the pelican) are juxtaposed on these capitals at Caen

49 (opposite) Panel of the type known as 'pierced'

48 The 'Attack on the Castle of Love' on this 14th-century mirror-case from Cologne is entirely symbolical; the 'virgins' are showering the knights with roses

is delivering a lady from the arms of a wild man of the woods, and is also seen receiving from the old guardian the keys of the castle in which the maidens are held captive. (Like the mirror-cases mentioned above, these caskets have by some authorities been attributed to Cologne, c 1340–50, and so continue the tradition of symbolism which was shown in the earlier reliquary caskets.)

If we seem to lay too much stress on these secular themes and objects, it is because they shed an interesting light on the history of ideas and help us to understand the spirit of the Middle Ages. Moreover, it is impossible not to be moved by the gracefulness and refinement of the heroes' figures, although a mirror-case in London [figure 24] shows that delicacy is not inconsistent with power. These pieces were pigmented, and one finds traces of colour on them, but as they were naturally subjected to a great deal of handling, the colours have generally been rubbed off.

In these works, unlike the religious pieces which reflect the styles of full-sized sculpture, one can see that the ivory carver has created something new which has itself affected full-sized sculpture, as witness the piers in the cathedrals of Lyons and Rouens, and the capitals in the Church of St Pierre at Caen [figure 47]. We find on the caskets episodes from romances which the ivory carvers helped to propagate, and which were to figure again on Italian pieces. Finally, it is of the utmost interest that they represent probably the latest full manifestation of the persistence of a symbolic language beginning in earliest times with the Venuses and cave-paintings of the prehistoric era. The accumulation of these symbols on casket-lids must always be referred to a magic context; they are emblems of inviolability aimed at defending the treasures within them, and it is logical that caskets containing jewels to convert a woman into a goddess should depict obstacles to the realization of perfect love.

Consideration of the very different style of Italian caskets and mirror-cases brings up the name of the Embriachi.

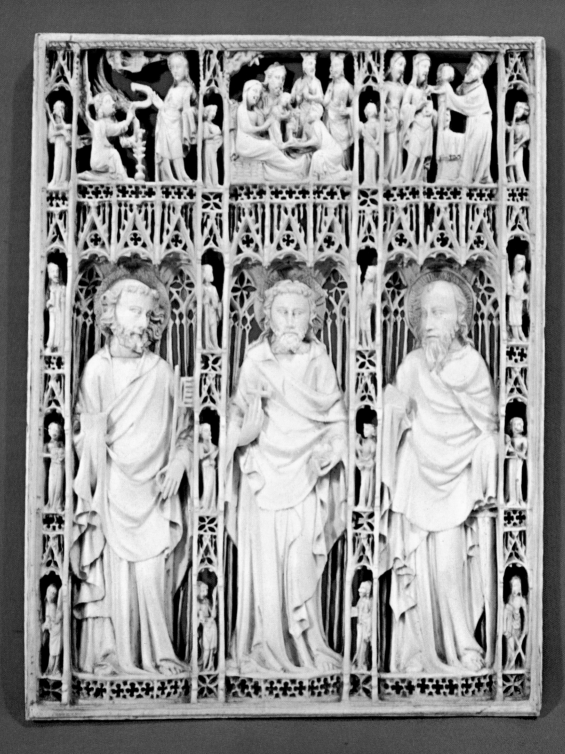

50 Marriage casket from the Embriachi school showing the story of Pyramus and Thisbe

These were intermediaries rather than creative artists, of Venetian extraction, who flourished at the end of the fourteenth century. They were responsible mainly for marriage caskets, whose destination is visible in their double escutcheons borne by nude figures, once painted but now plain. They became very fashionable, and as the nobility preferred them to French pieces, the latter became scarce or imitated the Italian designs during the fifteenth century.

Some church treasuries and museums include oblong examples [figure 51], but for the most part they took different shapes: square, hexagonal [figure 50] or even octagonal; they differ from French caskets in having prismatic, incurved lids ornamented with marquetry. Some were also made of coloured paste; small blocks of bone were always used, and as with French caskets, the sides were covered in scenes of gallantry and romance, such as episodes from Pyramus and Thisbe, and, from Boccaccio, the Marquis of Saluzzo, or the story of Griselda. But instead of a scholarly use of symbolical scenes we are given the chief events in lively narrative form. These caskets are to be found in all the museums of Europe, in the Museo Correr at Venice, in Berlin and Paris (Louvre, Cluny, Bibliothèque Nationale, etc).

Most of the mirror-cases are circular in shape like the French examples. As with the caskets, the scenes are depicted in a more rural setting among more numerous trees than in the earlier French examples, and although in comparison with the French the figures are hardly more than sketched, the impressionist technique itself is not without interest. It consists of scoring the entire surface so that it catches the light. Mirror-cases of similar workmanship were also made in France around the turn of the century [figure 54]. Another sort of mirror-case—octagonal, pierced in the centre over the metal plaque serving as mirror, and furnished with a handle — appeared in Italy in the fifteenth century, and was more closely related to retables than caskets; the carved bone decoration was combined with marquetry and they

51 A casket in the Embriachi style. The scenes show the story of Jason,
based on Benoit de Sainte-Maure's *Roman de Troie*

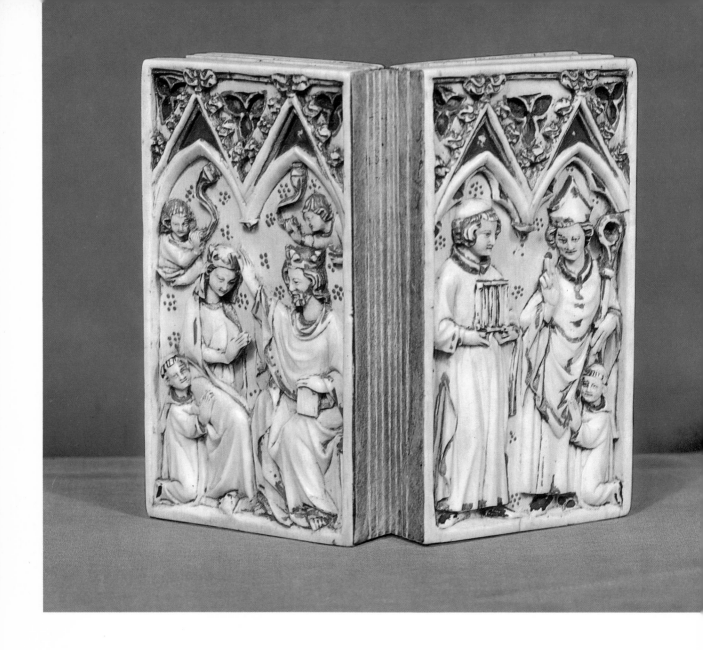

52 and 53 Writing-tablets from East France or the Rhineland
(14th century). On the outside are the Coronation of the Virgin,
a saintly bishop, St Lawrence and his gridiron; inside are six tablets,
originally coated with wax but later painted

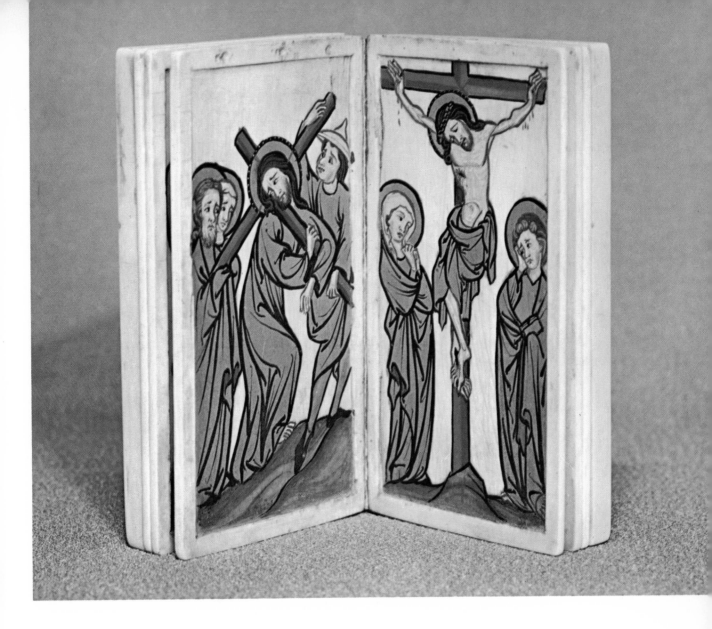

54 French mirror-case (c 1400), perhaps of Italian workmanship; this differs from earlier French secular ivories in that the figures are in contemporary costumes

were crowned by a pediment of the type seen in retables.

French mirror-cases followed the Italian pattern during the Renaissance, although circular cases were still being made, but now supplied with a handle; French carvers, of course, used ivory. The more relaxed handling of the figures, the rustic background, the use of marquetry, polychromy and bone, precious metals and gilding, all characterized caskets of the latter part of the fifteenth century, made by Flemish or Italian craftsmen working in the north of France or in Flanders, who were also responsible for retables. The Victoria and Albert Museum [figure 25] and the Louvre possess several examples with pictures of tournaments, dances and 'wild men'.

French, German, and Italian work shows that there was a new movement in the art of ivory, and this was the beginning of an international style. Spain seems to have remained quite outside it. French pieces were sent there, and many of them are found in church treasuries. The Spanish expressed their taste for bright colours by exaggerating their polychromy and setting them with precious stones. All their own most interesting work of this period is in the oriental tradition. It is the Moorish or Mozarabic (European under Moorish rule) style which characterizes their horns and caskets, which are often very sumptuous. Shallow relief and a surface entirely covered with patterns are their chief characteristics. We see little essential difference in style if we compare the mid-tenth century cylindrical box in the Louvre, made for a son of Abd ar-Rahman III and decorated with animals and horsemen, or the similar box of the same date in the Victoria and Albert Museum, made for Ziyad ibn Aflah, both from Cordoba, with the works of a century and more later from Cuenca and elsewhere. A similar style is also found in other regions under Moorish influence, like Sicily [figure 26]; the richly coloured and decorated Siculo-Arabic caskets are sometimes carved with Christian themes.

Apart from mirror-cases, the foregoing objects, whether

secular or religious, were fairly complicated, and usually made from a number of ivory plaques joined together. Diptychs and statuettes of saints were simpler, and while the large output of diptychs helped to spread the French style, the statuettes of saints came as much from other countries as from France. To the diptych (a religious object, since it was the most economic form of portable altar) we must add plaquettes covering writing-tablets; these were utilitarian, and their decoration was more secular than religious.

Diptychs generally combined together scenes from the Childhood and Passion of Christ, and Koechlin classes them according to their architectural setting, columns or arcades, or by the fact that the bands separating the different scenes were ornamented with roses. This is the case with the panel of a diptych illustrated in figure 32, in a fairly sophisticated style, where we see the star of the Magi mixed with roses, whereas in another illustrated panel [figure 55] arcades surround the rather more naively rendered scenes. Some splendid diptychs in the fifteenth-century style deal movingly with the cycle of the Passion alone.

Genuine English diptychs [figures 29 and 59] are few, but of extremely high quality. The setting is different; a flattened ogival arch appears here sooner than it did in France and is associated with crocketing. The design of roses is also common and has led to the identification of these diptychs as English. This is a more masculine than feminine art. Christ is often represented on judgement day. He is always more emphasized than the Virgin, and looks dignified and serious. Another class of ivories, known as 'pierced diptychs' [figure 49], have been ascribed to England, but it is much more likely that they are Milanese work of the early fifteenth century; many of these include a great number of architectural motifs, especially crenellations (unknown in French pieces), and they have an iconography of their own.

Diptychs must not be confused with plaquettes for covering writing-tablets. These plaquettes, generally illustrating

55 Left-hand panel of an 'arcaded' diptych. Below, the Nativity; above, the Holy Women at the Sepulchre

55

56 and 57 Two views of a group (Flanders or Germany, 15th century) probably inspired
by a German alabaster, with a Pietà on one side, Christ at Gethsemane on the other

58 Like retables and
diptychs, images of saints are
either didactic or take a
narrative form; thanks to
her confident faith,
St Margaret has defeated the
monster

59 An English diptych of the
mid-14th century

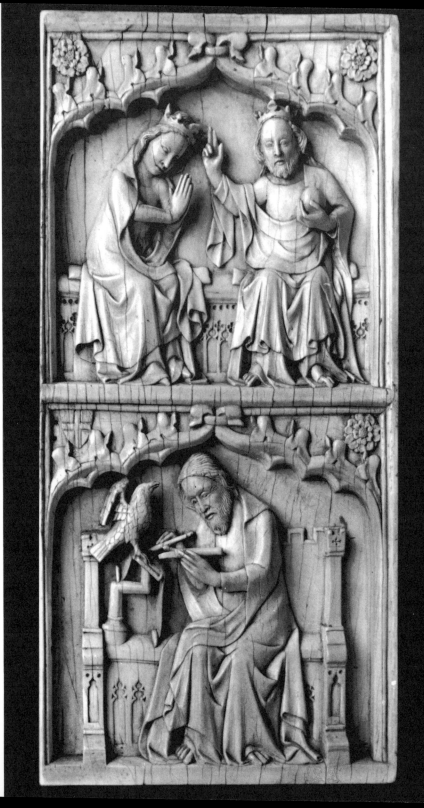

secular themes, served as a binding for a number of others designed to be covered with wax and written on with a style [figure 60]; two complete sets of writing-tablets of this sort, one containing six plaques afterwards embellished with paint [figures 52 and 53], can be seen in the Victoria and Albert Museum. The leaves of diptychs differ from tablet covers in that the former had a hinge on the inside edge, and the latter had holes at the top and sides, and compartments at the back to hold the plaques; these were hollow and surrounded by a shallow rim to contain the wax. A special guild of 'tablet-makers' made and sold these books of plaques.

Among religious objects, statuettes of Christ and the saints, and the more important groups, deserve special attention. Again, French work is outstanding, but mention must be made of English, Flemish and German ivories. The theme of the crucifixion seems to have been of little importance in France; one of the most beautiful, the Christ in the Homberg Collection, is English, while the Spanish Christ in the Cote Collection at Lyons is almost unbearably tragic. In England ivory carving runs parallel to alabaster work, also of excellent quality. Nothing could show this better than the two vertical groups of the Trinity illustrated in figures 34 and 35; the folds are softer in the ivory and some of the details are different: orb, dove, and crown. In contrast to the prettiness and mannered quality of French Gothic ivories, a Flemish group [figures 56 and 57] shows the moving quality of later medieval art. Side by side in a strangely distorted landscape, there are two scenes (Gethsemane and a Pietà) which might well have been inspired by the mystery-plays current at the time and also show the influence of engravings.

As usual, French carvers dealt most skilfully with feminine figures, such as the female saints: for example, the illustrated statuette of St Margaret triumphing over the dragon [figure 58]. The saint has an ecstatic expression and is giving thanks to heaven with her large hands, symbolical of her exceptional powers. She has defeated the dying

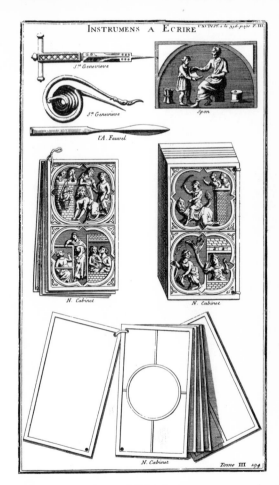

60 A plate from Montfaucon's *L'Antiquité Expliquée* (1719) showing the arrangement of writing tablets. The covers are decorated with secular subjects such as 'Virgil in his Basket'

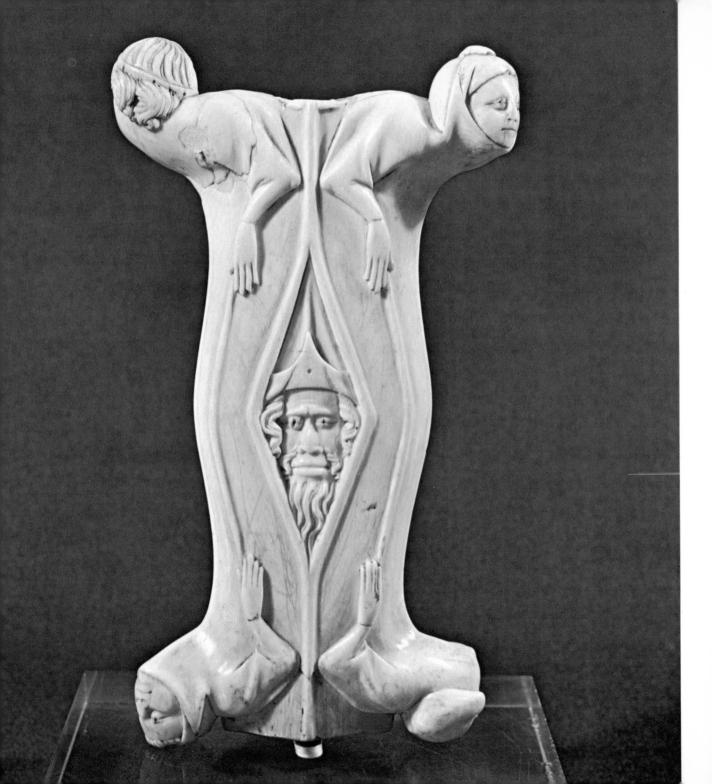

61 *(opposite)* The decoration of this French dagger-handle — two couples back to back on either side of a mask — is perhaps another variant of the tetramorphic image

62 A *gravoir* handle illustrating the 'Lay of Aristotle', a difficult but fairly normal subject for this class of objects (French, 14th century)

63 *(left)* St Catherine pointing to the Emperor Maximian, who has condemned her to torture by the wheel seen on the throne (French, 14th century)

64 *(opposite left)* Various bas-reliefs of this sort, carved in imitation of alabaster, have led to the identification of a separate Westphalian school

65 *(opposite right)* Pax (French, *c* 1500) bearing the name of 'Jehan Nicolle' and depicting St Roch above, St Sebastian below

monster. The polychromy deftly emphasizes the significant parts, such as hair, trimming on clothes, the gilded fur and large red nostrils and ears of the dragon, and the joint between the two pieces of ivory has been skilfully disguised by a gilded branch. French female saints are numerous and beautiful; they may be seated or standing, and St Catherine, the wise virgin, is often represented [figure 63]. St Catherine's image was often made in England as well, according to a text quoted by Dalton in his British Museum catalogue citing Alienore de Bohun (1322) who possessed one. But

male figures are always finer in England, as seen in the illustrated bust of a saintly king [figure 67], which is as noble as the bust of Christ from the same source.

In Italy, ivory carving was not much practised; the bas-relief in the Louvre showing St Jerome in the savage grandeur of his solitary surroundings bears comparison, however, with work by the best north Italian artists in bronze, such as Bellano. In Germany some rough work was done, very much in the style of their wood-carvings and bronzes, for instance, the bushy-haired St Christopher at Copenhagen, and a long

series of St Georges [figure 64] often imitating alabaster (M. Swarzenski, *Deutsche Alabasterplastik des XIV. Jahrhunderts*, 1921). The finest is copied from a goldsmith's piece and is in the Rothschild Collection. Spain alone made no essential contribution to this vast international concert, although a great many dubious pieces have been attributed to her, including pietàs and paxes, a class of object about which something must be said.

Paxes were, in fact, another type of religious object, whose workmanship specially reflected the cult of the saints. Already in the fourteenth century we find mention of many belonging to private individuals, churches, or princes; they continued being made until the beginning of the sixteenth century, but those we have are chiefly from the fifteenth. Consisting of a convex plaque usually with a silver handle, the pax was held out by the priest to be kissed by the faithful before communion; in Flanders, if two members of a family quarrelled, a pax was sent for to bring about a reconciliation. Paxes were not comparable in quality with the objects we have been describing, but their popular flavour makes them interesting and they teach us the iconography of the most venerated saints: St Roch and his dog, St Barbara and her tower. Two paxes survive which bear the names of Jehan Nicolle and Henri Lardenoi [figures 65 and 68], an unusual feature; these were at first thought to be the artists, but were certainly the owners. A Flemish pax [figure 69] was obviously inspired by wood-carving rather than engraving. The figures do not appear against a background of crossed lines as usual, but as if carved in the round against a hollowed-out background; in the Adoration of the Magi, Kaspar is a Negro, something one never sees in French ivories.

This study of the continuing Gothic tradition cannot conclude without some mention of episcopal croziers. Most of those we possess were made in France, and it was there that their iconography was determined. Generally speaking,

67 Bust of a saintly English king (14th century), as majestic as the figures of Christ of the same provenance

66 (*opposite*) Combs from the mid-15th century treat the same subjects as mirror-cases and caskets ('Fountain of Youth', etc), but with a new sense of the picturesque

the crook is decorated with vegetable themes: foliage, crocketing, sometimes ending in a dragon. Inside the spiral are figures carved in the round: on one side we see Christ on the cross between the Virgin and St John, on the other the Virgin in glory, with the infant Christ [figure 33]. Metal is often used in association with ivory; it may be mounted in copper, for instance.

Croziers from other countries hardly depart at all from this French formula. Thus a German crozier represents the same figures, but a young man has been added at the base of the staff; he appears to be threatening the dragon and is probably a newly baptized catechumen, saved by Christ's cross from the dragon, symbol of death. Italian croziers are distinguished by certain characteristics found also in other Italian artifacts: the importance given to vegetation as décor, particularly to crocketing, the multiplication of figures and scenes, polychromy, and the use of other materials with ivory.

With varying success, the different forms described carried on the medieval tradition beyond the end of the Middle Ages. But the Renaissance was to bring with it a far-reaching revolution, whose effects we must try to measure.

68 *(opposite)* Pax in the Italian style bearing the name of 'Henri Lardenoi' and depicting the Virgin crowned between St John the Baptist and St Barbara (French, 15th–16th century)

69 *(right)* Pax in the Flemish style depicting the Adoration of the Magi (French, 16th century)

# CHAPTER THREE

# Renaissance and Baroque Ivories

WE HAVE EXAMINED a series of religious and secular ivories showing the persistence of the Gothic tradition. This was evident principally in the architectural settings of gables, columns, and arcades; next, in the composition, and the use of a miniaturist's technique. Bas-relief was the chosen form, and edifying scenes were set side by side, as in cathedrals. Lastly, the statuettes of Virgins and saints and the croziers did not actually give the appearance of being carved in the round; they were meant to be looked at from the front, like the figures on the piers of cathedrals. By using single plaques, or fastening them together with metal hinges (caskets, diptychs, and retables), the ivory carver for the most part avoided having to join his pieces of ivory in order to get larger surfaces than the very limited ones provided by the nature of the material.

With the Renaissance everything changed; the fashion was no longer set by architecture and the architectural frame disappeared. Nor was it any longer a question of imitating miniatures or engraving. Sculpture and painting were now the models for ivory carvers to follow. In making large groups, tusks were cut lengthways; when necessary, several plaques were joined together. Thanks to an improved knowledge of anatomy, true carving in the round was achieved in the statuettes. By using lathes ivory was made to take on the most complicated shapes, and in relief as much

71 Falcon's hood-rest decorated with the *fleurs-de-lys* of France

70 (*opposite*) Religious subjects such as *Virtue Overcoming Vice* were taken as a pretext for powerful anatomical studies during the Italian Renaissance

trouble was taken over detail as over the general outline, in an attempt to achieve greater realism than previously, when some of the details used to be exaggerated to emphasize dogmatic significance or increase expressiveness.

But if, on the one hand, by forcing the stylistic bounds to the limit of the material, objects and groups of considerable dimensions were produced, the eighteenth century also produced innovations in very small works, or micro-reliefs, whether in the form of pierced-work, known in Dieppe as 'mosaic' and used particularly for shuttles, or in that of microscopic groups or landscapes on the covers of such objects as tobacco-jars. The Middle Ages had steered a course between these two extremes.

These developments were the result of the vigorous advances in painting and sculpture made during the Renaissance, which also imposed their patterns on the minor arts. And since it was in Italy that these arts shone most brilliantly, she supplanted France. We know that ivory was highly prized as a material, but it did not rank highest of all. It was not the kings by 'divine right', like the kings of France with their passion for display, who chose ivory to play an important part in the décor of their lives, but the lesser nobility, who were stifled in France but flourishing elsewhere. A general passion for Italy, contempt for the Middle Ages and a centralized monarchy produced a drastic transformation of all the medieval crafts in France − even a decline, as was the case with ivory. The few ivory carvers who remained, such as Van Opstal and Duquesnoy, were Flemish, Dutch, or Dieppois, for Dieppe was the only provincial centre where this craft continued to thrive throughout the eighteenth century (and even till the present day), because of her regular trade by sea with Africa.

It seems that secular ivory carving in France was getting very little encouragement from rich and noble patrons, as was happening elsewhere. That this patronage did exist is proved by certain Burgundian pieces like the 'oratory of the

72 *(opposite)* 13th-century Italian saddle-bow. The battle between amazons suggests a 'psychomachy', the struggle between virtues and vices

Duchesses', but we have already made clear that the treatment of secular objects like caskets and mirror-cases was impersonal and tells us nothing about their possessors, unlike the caskets made by the Embriachi or blazoned English diptychs.

In Italy, on the contrary, the few splendid pieces surviving from the Middle Ages show that noble patronage played an important part. Also, the number of rival cities must have created a more favourable atmosphere for ivory carving than France's political centralization. It is common knowledge that the Italian Renaissance was distinguished by the generous patronage of several families or personalities: the Medici in Florence, the Gonzaga in Mantua, and Pope Julius II. Most of the forms which were to be successful during this period came from Italy: mythological bas-reliefs (Brunswick Museum), statuettes, and medallions. But on the whole, Italy did not greatly value ivory, putting it far below

marble or even bronze. In the preceding period, as in the Renaissance, the finest artists had not been carvers of ivory. It is by no means certain that Giovanni Pisano and Benedetto da Majano really made the pieces attributed to them, any more than that the mythological statuettes attributed to Giovanni Bologna, Michelangelo, or Benvenuto Cellini in the last century were really by them. It is even possible, according to some authorities, that some of them are French.

Next to Italy, we must mention Flanders. More favourably situated for importing the material, she also created certain forms peculiar to the Renaissance, memento mori and rosary beads in particular.

73 A cantle from a Spanish or Sicilian saddle (early 14th century). The armorial bearings in the strapwork indicate that this object belonged to Frederick I, Prince of Aragon, King of Sicily

Germany's output during the seventeenth and eighteenth centuries was unequalled, both in the baroque and rococo styles. The same economic reasons apply here as in the Low Countries, for great quantities of ivory from India arrived at German ports just as they did at Antwerp and Amsterdam. We notice a Chinese influence in German ivories, as a result of the trade with the Far East. And, as in Italy, German and Austrian ivories could not have existed without noble, royal, or even imperial patronage (since power was shared between the various Electors) or even that of the wealthy middle classes of many of the cities.

The Germans were pleased by the malleability of the material and its easiness to carve. It is interesting to notice that some of the petty sovereigns worked as amateur ivory carvers; their example must have been contagious, for Peter the Great made a tobacco-jar from ivory. We know that the romantic, imaginative Germans were easily led into producing extremely complicated baroque or rococo ornament, particularly when they were in search of allegories or symbolism. Some ivories show this style carried to excess, for instance, the *Last Judgement* by Steinhart after Michelangelo. All the same, even if we make certain reservations about German carved plaques, a comparison of them with similar Italian or French work results to the advantage of the Germans, and teutonic frigidity diminishes our grounds for criticism. Nor can one sufficiently praise the magnificence and richness of their goblets of ivory and silver or silver-gilt, decorated with lively scenes from mythology; of their dishes and vases; the luxuriant display of monsters and animals on hunting-flasks, circular powder-flasks, handles for table knives, knives for cutting up stags, and daggers; and the savage beauty of the composite figures or forceful masks on cane-handles, reminiscent of memento mori.

In all these different genres there was nothing to impose constraint, except the dimensions and structure of the ivory plaque itself. Sinuous spirals, such as were seen on English

74 Although decorated with a representation of the game, this dice-box nevertheless comes from a cathedral treasure

'taus', are found again in these German works in inexhaustible abundance, and curiously enough, there is a link between their superimposed designs based on revolving wheels and the decorated columns of Romanesque, Languedocian, or even Mesopotamian doorways, just as in another way it is permissible to see in the subtle symbolism of French carved retables a continuation of Egyptian bas-reliefs and their juxtaposed themes. Many German crucifixes show their Romanesque descent, and their marvellous beauty and serene dignity are very far from the extravagances of Grünewald. A consummate understanding of dramatic organization, comparable to that displayed in the old Carolingian book-covers, can be seen in certain unbelievably magnificent altars, in which the ivory carvers accomplish on a miniature scale what Bernini had realized on a gigantic one.

While emphasizing the interest of German output, we must not neglect the initial impetus given by Italy, nor the works of Flemish rivals (reflecting the influence of that great lover of ivories, Rubens), nor the artisan-produced ivories of Dieppe and Paris, which sometimes bear the stylistic imprint of Watteau. However, we must first return to the Gothic period and deal with a series of pieces owing little to France, many of them coming from Italy, Germany, or the north. These foreshadow the Renaissance in several ways, either by their dimensions or treatment. And another reason why we should study them here is that many of these objects, such as chessmen, knife-handles, or to a lesser extent, combs, are the beginning of a series which was to continue throughout the period with which we are now concerned. Others, on the contrary, like whip-handles, belt-buckles, *gravoirs*, rests for falcons' hoods, and saddles (whose importance in aristocratic life and hunting ritual is revealed in secular ivories and romances) disappeared with the Middle Ages.

We are here essentially concerned with secular objects, and although some, such as combs, were abundantly made in

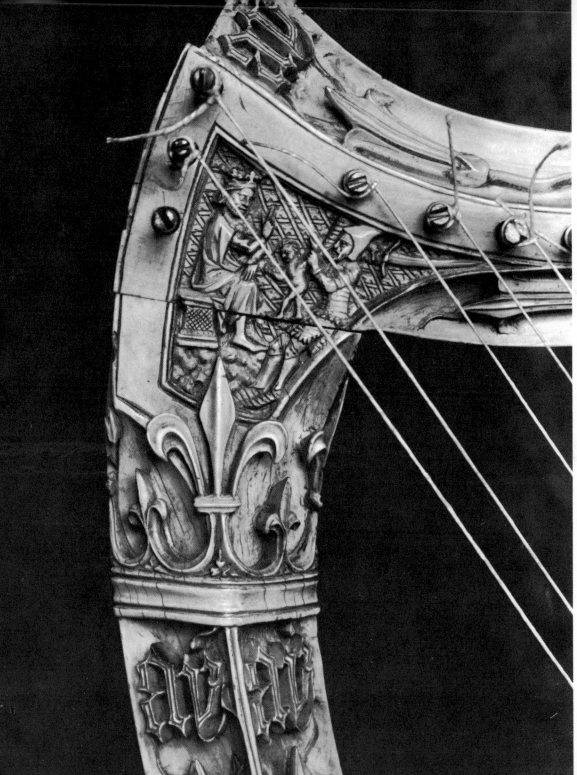

75 The Massacre
of the Innocents
is depicted on
the elbow of
this harp, pro-
bably from the
court of Savoy
or Burgundy.
On the other
side is the
Adoration of
the Magi, and
on the back is
the Nativity

75

France, they owed less to the Gothic genius than caskets and mirror-cases did, and were often emblazoned with coats of arms, unlike the latter. Unfortunately, only a few of these objects have come down to us for various reasons, above all because saddles, chessboards, and hunting-horns were not made of ivory alone, but with the addition of precious materials like gold, silver-gilt, enamel, cabochons, and jewels, and this certainly led to theft or damage.

Few saddles have survived, but they are remarkable for their magnificence. Their style, decoration, and the use of bone and marquetry identify them as Italian in origin. The German or French devices often ornamenting them tell us nothing about their origin, for it was one of the customs of chivalry to borrow mysterious devices from foreign lands. It is surprising that they should be made of ivory, but these were ceremonial saddles, intended for royal processions (Schlosser, *Elfenbein-Saettel des ausgehenden Mittelalters* XV vol. Jahrbuch, Vienna Museum). There are only about twenty in existence, to be found in various museums such as the Tower of London, the Wallace Collection, London, two in the Berlin Arsenal, three in the Budapest Museum, in Vienna, Florence, and Modena. The museum of the Paris Arsenal possesses a wooden one.

Most saddles date from the fourteenth century; one of the most beautiful, in the Possenti Collection, is fifteenth century. This and the Florence saddle are decorated with unicorn themes; on the others we see St George, wild men, or a lover's bestiary: lion, pelican, phoenix, mermaids. Other themes can be found in Romances; Chrétien de Troie tells us that the history of Aeneas and Troy was engraved on the saddle-bow of an ivory saddle, and a saddle belonging to Raoul, Comte d'Eu, bore the image of the God of Love.

Two accessories from ceremonial saddles have come down to us: a thirteenth-century saddle-bow [figure 72] and a fourteenth-century cantle [figure 73], made entirely of ivory of Italian workmanship, decorated with a tournament scene. The interlace borders are in the Romanesque tradition and the eagle on the cantle has heraldic significance, whereas the battle between Amazons on the saddle-bow is from the school of Nicola Pisano, according to Koechlin. Saddle-bow and cantle acted as curved supports to the saddle at back and front, the cantle serving as back-rest and therefore being the more important. In contrast to the French habit of carving a separate but often complicated theme on each piece of ivory, the width of the cantle forced the carver to use several plaques, but here he has carved a single subject on them, the tournament, treated with more simplicity than is usual in French pieces.

We shall deal rapidly with various objects belonging to a less important series. One often sees on both religious and secular ivories the figure of a servant whipping a horse, but no ivory whip-handles survive. We do, however, possess a few ivory falcons' hood-rests [figure 71], accessories of coursing which were also made in wood or bone. The falcon's hood used to be placed on these after the bird had been set free from the wrist of the servant who carried it, to swoop on its prey. They were decorated with the owner's arms on the

76 Like many medieval objects, this belt-buckle is decorated with religious subjects despite its secular use

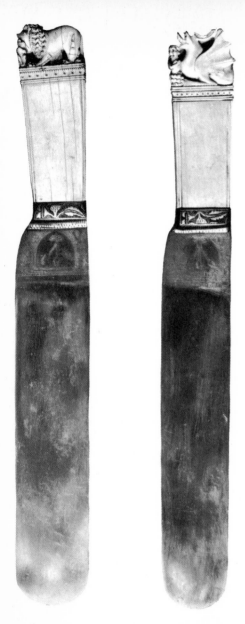

77 Italian knives from the 16th century; the handles are carved in a sober classical style

front, sometimes also with a motto. One in the Figdor Collection in Vienna bears the inscription, *nunc aut quondam*; it dates from the sixteenth century, but the design has not changed with the course of time. The *Hunting Book* of Frederick I shows us a hood on its rest. The example in Florence is German, but they were also made in Italy.

There is much documentary proof of the great variety of musical instruments in use during the Middle Ages, and some of these, such as harps, must have been made of ivory. However, hardly any instruments from this period have survived, almost the only one being in fact a harp [figure 75]. It is made of an upright and a cross-piece pierced with twenty-five holes for the strings; these are divided into a series of compartments decorated with the letters A and Y and *fleurs de lys*. Various suggestions have been made about these initials, which probably allude either to Amadeus IX of Savoy and Yolande of France (*d.* 1478) or to Antoine de Bourgogne and Isabelle de Luxembourg (*Aultre n'auray*). This extremely interesting object demonstrates the internationalism of art at the end of the Middle Ages.

A few belt-buckles from the end of the Middle Ages have also survived [figure 76]. This example is in the Archeological Museum at Ghent; the Saint Césaire specimen is an early imitation of barbarian bronze-work. People have been puzzled to find religious subjects, saints or a skull on these secular objects; however, this is to forget the holiness attached in the Middle Ages to the virtue these belts were supposed to defend. We also possess only a single candlestick, in spite of the fact that the medieval lantern-maker's guild was an important one; it is in the museum at Saint Omer, and is decorated with a scene in high relief, which has sometimes been interpreted as the judgement of Paris, sometimes as the marriage of the King of Murcia's daughter, from a romance. It consists of two parts: a circular foot, on whose wide border the figures are carved, and above it a tube and ring to hold the candle.

78 French spoons from the 17th century: the Three Graces and the Whore of Babylon on the Seven-Headed Beast of the Apocalypse

79 Ceremonial carving knife from France, showing Italian influence (15th century)

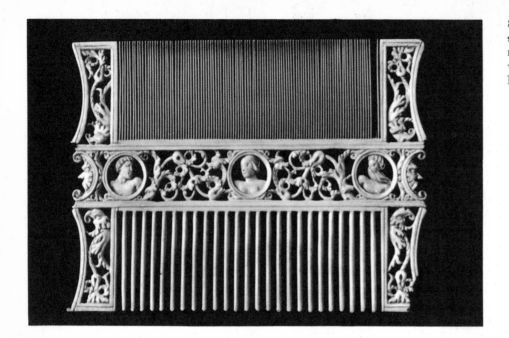

A proof of the inter-penetration of the secular and religious spheres is that we possess a considerable number of dice-boxes from the end of the Middle Ages, decorated, of course, with secular themes [figure 74], but preserved only by being included among church treasures. This is true of the specimen in Münster Cathedral, on which are themes illustrating the Nine Champions, Aristotle and Campaspe, and Samson and Delilah. The treasure in the Duomo in Milan includes another example, decorated with representations of the liberal arts. The rarity of such subjects in French art, and the likeness between the example at Vannes and works in the Embriachi tradition, lead one to suppose that these objects were not made in France. They were to be followed by dice-boxes made of bone and quite without artistic value.

There was another important series of objects, however, whose development can be traced as far as the Renaissance

81 Complicated chessmen of Morse ivory, each made up of several figures, which testify to the survival of a very old tradition and also reveal the military spirit animating this game

82 Chessman from northern Europe
(13th century), made from a walrus tusk

83 Early medieval draughts piece, thought to be a representation of Hera and the infant Heracles

and even later. Parallel to works by the Embriachi, but for the most part superior in style, we find the Italians making *gravoirs*, objects possibly used for parting the hair, which vanished at the end of the Middle Ages. The original decorations on their handles show a definite relationship to those on dagger or knife-handles and ceremonial carving-knives, the latter also of Italian origin. The style thus created was the starting-point of a fashion which was to persist throughout the seventeenth century in France and Germany. Following the Romanesque tradition that we have seen thriving in Italy, particularly in the decoration of saddles, man is represented struggling with monsters, gryphons, and dragons, and at the same time caught in a tangle of foliage. This is applicable to several *gravoirs* in the Louvre, while others show us the amorous scenes we expect from secular French ivories: rides in the forest (the usual setting for the 'adventures' in Romances), couples embracing, or the story of Aristole [figure 62].

There are French dagger-handles in existence, decorated with religious themes of standing saints, generally crude in

84 (*opposite*) Knight from a set of 14th-century chessmen, probably from England

85 and 86 Two views of a rosary bead from Flanders, where similar
designs appear on the heads of canes. The three heads, representing
Woman, Death and Christ, show that the flesh dies without Christ's help

87 The influence of Mantegna is clearly apparent in this Italian bas-relief illustrating one of Petrarch's *Trionfi*, the 'Triumph of Fame'

style, and some fine examples, such as an early one from the Victoria and Albert Museum [figure 61] showing two couples back to back. But the more important pieces, such as ceremonial carving-knives [figure 79], show us lions and monsters alongside classical scenes of gallantry or hunting, either in the French or Italian style. We find these lions and dragons ornamenting the ends of cutlery handles of classic design made during the Italian Renaissance [figure 77], and amorous or monstrous scenes on French baroque handles of the seventeenth century [figure 78], not to mention the wild fantasies issuing from the teutonic imagination, to which we shall return later.

Why should we find these amorous scenes (three Graces, etc), on spoons? And why these alarming monsters on the other hand? In the monasteries, images from the Apocalypse were sometimes hung in refectories, while Jean Cassien's *Collations*, the story of the adventures of the ascetics of the Thebaid, would be read aloud during the meal. This was a way of reminding the monks of the precariousness of man's fate at the very moment when they were about to enjoy the only pleasure allowed to them. The menacing monsters, lions in particular, come from Romanesque iconography, and probably have a similar significance; allusions to the Apocalypse can also sometimes be seen on cutlery handles. In the old days, meals followed a ritual, and carving the meat was the particular prerogative of the master of the house. So that it was not only the design of the handles that had to be symbolic, but also the colours of the materials they were made from; the King of France used ebony handles in Lent, ivory ones at ordinary times, and handles of ebony and ivory combined at Pentecost (*Comptes de l'argenterie des rois de France d'Etienne de la Fontaine*, fourteenth century).

It is symptomatic that, except for some liturgical examples, we have hardly any medieval combs [figure 66]. These objects continued to be made after the Middle Ages,

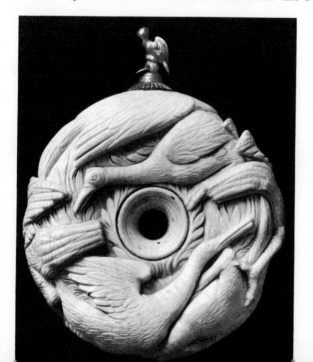

89 Antler-shaped powder flask from France or the southern Netherlands (17th century)

88 (*left*) German powder flask of the late 17th century

87

90 *(right)* One of the few 16th-century rosaries that have survived intact, made up of eleven beads of unequal size (Flanders or northern France)

91 *(opposite)* Coin cabinet by Angermayr from the early 17th century. The incredibly rich decoration, which derives from the Italian Renaissance, does not interfere with the clarity of the composition

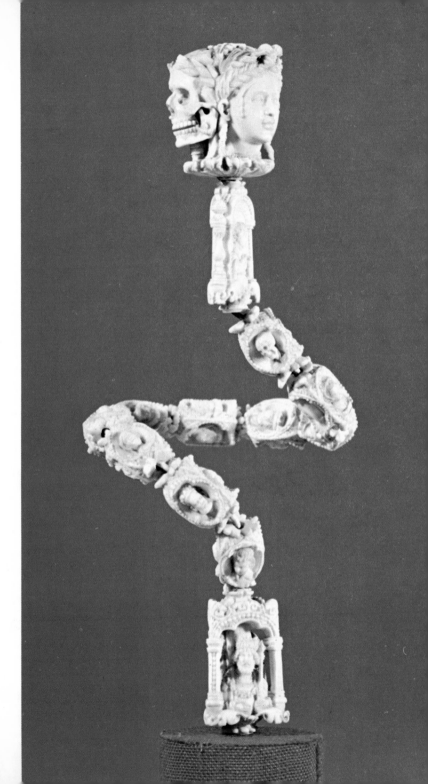

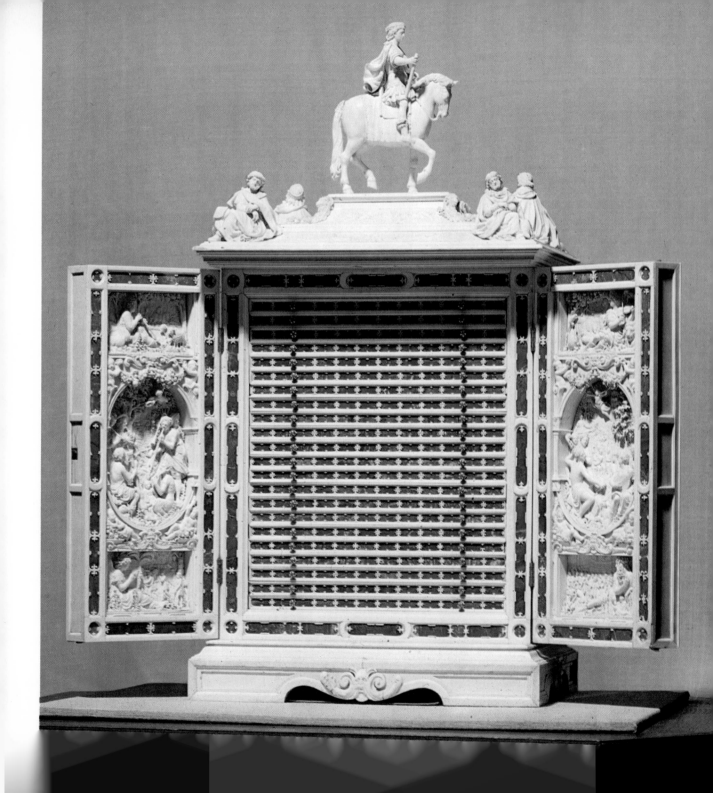

and those we possess come chiefly from the end of the fifteenth century or the Renaissance [figure 80]. Yet there is every indication that this craft was of prime importance in the Middle Ages. In fact, it seems that the term *pignier* (comb-maker) was ordinarily used to describe ivory carvers in general, indicating that those who made *pignières*, or cases of toilet articles, went on to make other ivory objects. The backs of medieval liturgical combs were decorated with oriental designs and there was only one row of teeth. They were used to disentangle tonsured heads of hair, whereas ordinary combs had two rows of teeth, one fine and one coarse, on opposite sides of the spine.

In the fifteenth century, liturgical combs were made to the same design as secular combs and these are to be found in some church treasuries, for example, at Reims. Religious themes sometimes appear on ordinary combs. During the Renaissance ivory combs were made in Germany as well as in Flanders, and with a new repertory: Paris and the three Graces and David and Bathsheba were themes designed to show female nudes to advantage, and were framed in Italian grotesques.

But of all secular objects, the most durable and best represented in the museums, with contributions from all over Europe, are the chessmen. In medieval times, the church had to take all social classes to task for their passion for games of chance, and we read of the sumptuousness of chess-boards and tables. There were sixteen pieces a side: king, queen, bishops, knights, castles and pawns. It would take us outside the scope of this work to study their changing forms, which included oriental animals like elephants and camels, for the game undoubtedly came from India. Northern European chessmen were made from walrus ivory [figure 82], and they retained the traditional forms from the eleventh century right down to the seventeenth; the figures are roughly shaped, massive, celtic, and of barbaric beauty. An important discovery on the Isle of Lewis in the

92 *(opposite)* Flemish tobacco-grater, representing the figure of a doctor (17th century)

93 *(below)* The rich decoration on this German game dish by Johann Michael Maucher (*d.* 1646) is comparable to Palissy pottery and displays scenes inspired by Ovid's *Metamorphoses*

94 (*opposite*) Portrait medallion of
Georg Johann IV of Saxony by
Balthasar Permoser (*d.* 1732), who was
also an important sculptor in stone.
The treatment of flesh, wig, cloth and
armour is admirably differentiated

95 (*left*) This altar by Dötebeer
(south Germany) reflects the Gothic
tradition. The graceful group of the
fainting Virgin inside a baroque
frame is clearly inspired by Roger
van der Weyden's *Descent from the
Cross*

94

Hebrides showed us how interesting this craft was (Madden, *Historical Remarks*, 1832).

To the chessmen we must add the round pieces used in backgammon [figure 83]. A curiously archaic form to be found in several museums is that of a castle defended by a crowd of knights, or a bishop surrounded by clergy [figure 81]. In the south of Europe these static and archaic designs came to life; the most famous of such pieces is the knight in the Ashmolean Museum at Oxford [figure 84], and later in the fifteenth century the pieces adopted the armour and clothes worn in contemporary warfare.

The contribution made by the Italian Renaissance was not only seen in the development of small objects. An example of mythological bas-relief [figure 87] appears on two hexagonal reliquaries from Graz in Styria, illustrating the six triumphs of Petrarch, probably the work of a maker of bronzes from Mantua or Verona in the circle of Mantegna. Among the most famous statuettes in the round, the Holofernes, or Goliath, in the museum in Liverpool must be mentioned. The group entitled *Virtue Overcoming Vice* [figure 70] is a good example of the new vigour displayed by these works. Giovanni Bellini, Valerio Belli and Bernardo de Castel Bolognese probably carved in ivory as well as in rock crystal. In the same way, the medallion, an Italian form, was an imitation of the medal form.

Italy was not alone in setting the fashion for imitating bronze, marble, cameos or precious metals by means of a gleaming polished surface and firmness of line. We must not forget the memento mori, or rosary beads, whose curious iconography, exemplifying the new technique, has been studied by English experts (F. Parker-Weber, *Aspects of Death*, 1918). In this genre Germany made hideous death's heads devoured by worms and serpents, and France charming heads, while Flanders was the most prolific of all in creating strings of heads [figures 85 and 86]; in some necklaces four heads representing love and death were set side by

97 *Fainting Christ Supported by Angels*, by the Bavarian carver, Andreas Faistenberger (c 1646–1735), after Campagna and Michelangelo

96 (opposite) *Fainting Christ Supported by Angels*, by the 17th-century Flemish artist, Faidherbe, after Campagna and Michelangelo

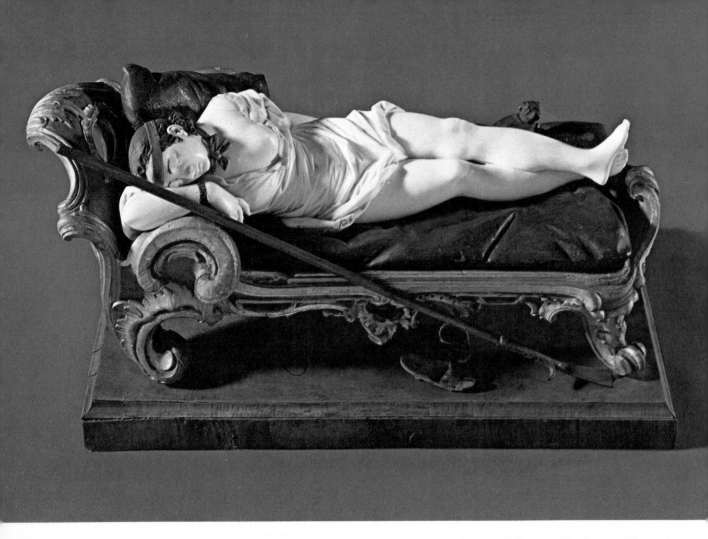

98 J. C. W. von Lücke's exquisitely sensual *Sleeping Shepherdess.* The artist was well known as a modeller in porcelain as well as an ivory carver

side. There are several complete strings of beads of this sort in existence [figure 90] (Petit Palais, Paris, and Victoria and Albert Museum).

Although German work bore the stamp of medieval tradition, it also contributed to the great artistic revival of the Renaissance by imitating the works of famous painters and sculptors. Dürer's monogram is seen on two female nudes in the National Bavarian Museum, and a bas-relief of a battle in the Musée de Cluny is signed by Hans Sebald Beham and dated 1545.

New sorts of objects appeared. First, powder-flasks [figure 89]. These receptacles, generally bifurcated like a stag's antler, were intended to contain the very fine powder used in portable arms with wheel-locks, and they continued in use until 1748. The flat surface allowed room for scenes to be carved – mainly of mythological subjects in France and Italy – and religious ones, such as the Trinity or Resurrection, in Germany or Russia. Powder-flasks of classical design were also made of ivory in France, and from Germany came some like flat bottles with metal necks. On the former Italian grotesques would be seen, like those of Diane de Poitiers' knife, as it is called, or the famous hunting-horn in the Rothschild Collection. German examples displayed a more realistic art inspired by hunting [figure 88].

Secondly, we must mention tobacco-graters. These little utensils, used by snuff-takers to grate a plug of tobacco, were often made of ivory and consisted of two ivory valves enclosing a metal grater. They were often decorated with charmingly fantastic figures; two sixteenth-century graters from Dieppe show us a woman in Norman costume of the period, and a snuff-taker with a rat biting his throat (indicating the proper punishment for his vice), while Flemish graters display genre figures [figure 92].

These objects, many of which date from the eighteenth century, owe little to Italy, for the international current set in motion at the Renaissance was to sweep on into the

99 Portrait medallion of the Princess Palatine, (Dieppe, 17th century) by Filie

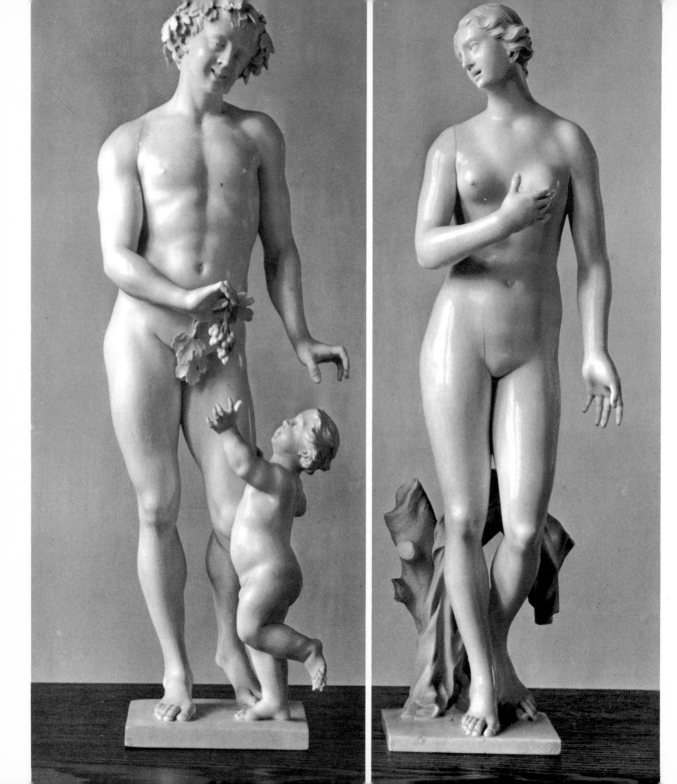

baroque period. Germany regained the supremacy she had had earlier, during the Carolingian and Romanesque periods, and this was to a large extent due to the active patronage of some of the Prince-Electors, for instance, Georg Wilhelm, Elector of Brandenburg (in 1640) or his successor, Maximilian, himself an amateur carver and the creator of a satyr's mask supporting two candlesticks, which is not without merit (National Bavarian Museum). After him came Ferdinand Maurice (*d.* 1679) and Maximilian III, both of whom also made candlesticks, while Rudolf II, Emperor of Austria, was the pupil of Peter Zick, an ivory carver from Nuremberg.

Among the important centres, Dresden and Bavaria must be mentioned. In Dresden Augustus the Strong, Elector of Saxony and King of Poland, had the celebrated 'Zwinger' decorated by the sculptor, Permoser, an ivory carver of the first rank, and attracted other ivory workers too. Even foreign ivory carvers were summoned to these courts. Johann Wilhelm, Elector of the Palatinate, sent for Antonio Leoni, a Venetian carver of the early eighteenth century, fellow-pupil and rival of Elhafen. Francis van Bossuit, an Italianized Flemish carver, rival of Faidherbe, went to the court of Augustus Wilhelm of Brunswick (1714–31). A Dutchman, Jacob Zeller, carried out a labour of great patience for the Elector of Saxony in 1620, by making a frigate complete in every detail after the manner of the junks made by the Chinese. As in other countries, craftsmen belonging to other guilds, sculptors like Permoser, goldsmiths and enamellers from Dresden and Danzig like Krüger and Keller, or local workers in amber, often worked at the same time as ivory carvers.

There is no doubt that during the prolific epoch which saw the triumph of baroque the greatest number of professional ivory carvers was to be found in Germany; whole dynasties practised the craft, from father to son, for instance, the Zick family at Nuremberg and the Lückes at Kassel. In Germany an entirely original art developed, with its own

100 and 101 *(opposite) Bacchus and Venus* by Elhafen

characteristic objects, such as goblets, beer mugs, game dishes; things that would be made in other countries of nobler materials like marble or bronze – allegorical statuettes in the style of garden statuary, altar-pieces, figures of sovereigns vanquishing their enemies – were all made by the Germans in ivory.

However, Italian influence remained paramount throughout the seventeenth century. It is shown in the sumptuous game dishes [figure 93], sometimes lavishly decorated with mythological scenes; there is an example by the Flemish carver Coppe, pupil of Guglielmo della Porta, also with illustrations from Ovid's Metamorphoses, and another in the National Museum at Münich with biblical and mythological scenes, Romulus and Remus, etc. Italian influence is clearly visible in the work of the Bavarian, Christoph Angermayr (d. 1632), a native of Wallheim and the author of bas-reliefs reminiscent of Raphael.

Angermayr's masterpiece, and perhaps the masterpiece of all German ivory carving, is the coin cabinet with medallions

102 and 103 Details from *The Triumph of the Cross* (c 1710) by Permoser, a group which can be linked to works by Bernini (tombs at St Peter's or the *Ecstasy of St Theresa* at S Maria della Vittoria) or Legros (the altar of the Gesù)

104 *(right)* Crucifix from St Martin-du-Bois, France, period of Louis XIII

105 *(opposite) Crucifixion* by Rauchmiller (1645–1686)

[figure 91], made between 1618 and 1624 in collaboration with Peter Candid for the wife of the Elector Frederick IV. The coin cabinet is less than three feet high by eighteen inches wide, but it is decorated all over. On top there is a Roman Emperor on horseback among four prostrate figures representing conquered races; on the doors are high reliefs within an architectural frame reminiscent of the early Renaissance and its revival of classical forms. As in the allegorical style popular under Louis XIV, the subjects chosen

103

(Orpheus charming animals, Apollo, Romulus and Remus, etc) indirectly flatter the sovereign who restored peace. On top of the doors are two genii holding the arms of Bavaria and Lorraine.

Italian influence is shown in a curious manner in religious or mythological bas-reliefs. The Christ supported by two angels on the altar of San Giuliano at Venice (by Girolamo Campagna after Michelangelo's Pietà in the Duomo at Florence) inspired both the Bavarian Faistenberger [figure 97] and Lucas Faidherbe, a Flemish pupil of Rubens [figure 96]. The German work, with its architectural frame, the languid figure of the Christ, and the faces of the angels is closer to Italy in spite of its greater coldness and sculptural rigidity. The Flemish work is more pictorial, the attitudes more true to life, and the details more realistic.

The best artists in ivory were trained in the schools of Italian masters and their dependence becomes clear in their bas-reliefs and statuettes. Ignaz Elhafen (1656–1716) lived at first in Rome, where he worked under Dutch artists as a fellow-pupil of Antonio Leoni; later he joined the school of Bernini. In 1685 he was in Vienna; next he was summoned to Düsseldorf by the Elector Johann Wilhelm of the Palatinate, whose sister he married, proving in what high consideration his guild was held. His bas-reliefs represented the rape of the Sabines, Diana and Callisto, the judgement of Paris and battle-scenes, but they were not as good as his statuettes [figures 100 and 101].

Balthasar Permoser (1651–1732), the Dresden carver, also served his apprenticeship in Italy, where he spent fourteen years; he worked alternately in Florence for Cosimo III and in Dresden. In Berlin he worked as a sculptor in the Charlottenburg park, for he was as skilful with stone, wood, and metal as he was with ivory. He excelled at portrait medallions [figure 94], a genre which spread from Italy all over Europe, particularly after 1650. His rivals in this field were J. Dobbermann at Dresden and the Lückes at Kassel, or French carvers such as Jean Cavalier, who worked at all the courts of Europe, le Marchand, a carver from Dieppe who worked mainly in England, and their contemporaries [figure 99]. Permoser also carved mythological figures, allegories of seasons and gods, Ceres, Flora, Bacchus, and Winter after Michelangelo (his *Summer* and *Spring* were used as models for porcelain), *Mercury Arising and Argus Asleep*, and the group known as *Hercules, Omphale, and Cupid*.

Permoser's masterpiece is an alterpiece, a group nearly four feet high, entitled the *Triumph of the Cross*, in the Ratsbibliothek at Leipzig [figures 102 and 103]. Christ is surrounded by an aureole, the cross stands on a copper globe above a hideously grinning skull, the serpent is threatening Eve, Satan is writhing in convulsions, and some innocent children are playing. Permoser's altarpiece was bound to be imitated, and so it was, in private altars in central Europe. Meanwhile, another altar, Dötebeer's in the Berlin Museum, is much closer to the Gothic tradition [figure 95].

Permoser's successor at the court of Weimar in 1732 was Johann Christoph Wolfgang von Lücke, a native of Schwerin. He executed a famous crucifix made of only two pieces of ivory. German crucifixes are certainly the most beautiful, although no other form of ivory carving was so widespread in Europe. In spite of the obvious kinship between the attitudes and types of Christs and crosses, it is easy to feel the difference between a unique work of art and one of a series. Compare, for instance, Mathias Rauchmiller's crucifix (reminiscent of Lücke's) and that at Saint-Martin du Bois

106 *(opposite) St Jerome and the Lion* by the 18th-century sculptor, Theophilus Wilhelm Freese, whose work is notable for its realism

107 *(right)* The artist of this *St Sebastian*, signed 'I.P.H.F.' was possibly Petel, a pupil of Rubens, who executed the same subject in wood

[figures 104 and 105], a French work. Yet many of the French crucifixes were highly esteemed by their contemporaries: some were made in the Saint-Claude district (Jaillot, Villerme); Jean Guillermin's at Lyons was famous; another, signed M. A. and believed to be by Michelangelo, was actually by M. Anguier, and so on.

Lücke was also the author of medallions, 'scientific' objects, and works designed to be carried out in porcelain rather than ivory. In fact, he began his artistic career as Director of Design at Meissen (1728–29), nor did he afterwards abandon this activity, whether in Vienna, in Fürstenberg or Schleswig. His charming polychrome *Sleeping Shepherdess* [figure 98], of which there is a copy in Flensburg porcelain at the court of Denmark (1754), shows how much he had learned from practising this closely related art.

A list of all the German ivory carvers of the seventeenth and eighteenth centuries, professional or otherwise, would not be very interesting. It is more profitable to point out what they had in common. Whether they were depicting saints, gods, biblical characters, St Jerome [figure 106], St Sebastian [figure 107], Venus, Bacchus, the rape of Deianira [figure 108], Adam and Eve, or Christ on the cross, they made their subjects the excuse for admirable anatomical studies, in which each carver expressed his own temperament: Freese realistically, Schlüter forcefully, Petel with sometimes realistic peasant robustness, Elhafen with a sort of pagan idealism. As these statuettes were reduced in size, they were placed on a dark pedestal, which contrasted with the whiteness of the ivory.

The beautiful bodies of ancient divinities made a procession round the bellies of tankards, goblets and beer mugs, or even of Flemish salt-cellars. There is a magnificent one by the Augsburg goldsmith, Bernard Straus, probably inlaid with silver by Conrad Wickert [figure 119]; more modest artifacts were also made at Augsburg [figure 109]. These splendid objects were ordered by foreign sovereigns; the

109 Augsburg beer-mug (17th century), bacchic theme with children and lions

108 *(opposite)* This beautiful *Rape of Deianira*, formerly attributed to Rauchmiller, is the work of an unknown Austrian artist.
Its realism is particularly evident in the veins in the horse's body of the centaur and the expression of the crying child

specimen made of silver-gilt and ivory in the Bibliothèque
Nationale belonged to Sobieski. The subjects were adapted to
the objects, for in classical times hydromel was believed to
assure immortality to the Gods and it is known how highly
prized drinking-horns always were by the Teutons.

The decoration of tankards was not purely Germanic; on
some of the most beautiful we see the influence of Rubens
and his school, while a frequently reappearing theme on
Flemish salt-cellars of similar shape [figure 110] is the
*Procession of Silenus*, the subject of a picture ascribed to Van
Dyck in the Brussels museum [figure 111]. These imitations
of Rubens have resulted in many tankards being attributed
to Faidherbe, who was admittedly one of Rubens' pupils, but

so far without definite proof. Others may well be from the hand of the German, Petel. Rubens was the patron of many ivory carvers, for he had a great taste for such objects, and the painting of his studio by Cornelis de Beaulieu [figure 112] in the Pitti Gallery, Florence, shows us an ivory statuette of Aphrodite of Cnidus belonging to him, standing on a cabinet (Van Bever, *Les tailleurs d'ivoire de la Renaissance à nos jours*, 1946).

The variety of artifacts was very great; thus in the eighteenth century, ivory objects were used to illustrate the

110 *(opposite left)* Ivory vessel designed like a goblet, a work which has been attributed to both Faidherbe and Petel

111 *(opposite right) Procession of Silenus,* a painting attributed to Van Dyck, which inspired the carver of figure 110 through the medium of an engraving (the figures are reversed)

112 *Rubens's Art Collection* by Cornelis de Beaulieu, showing an ivory statuette standing on a cabinet. Rubens's will shows that he possessed many ivory objects

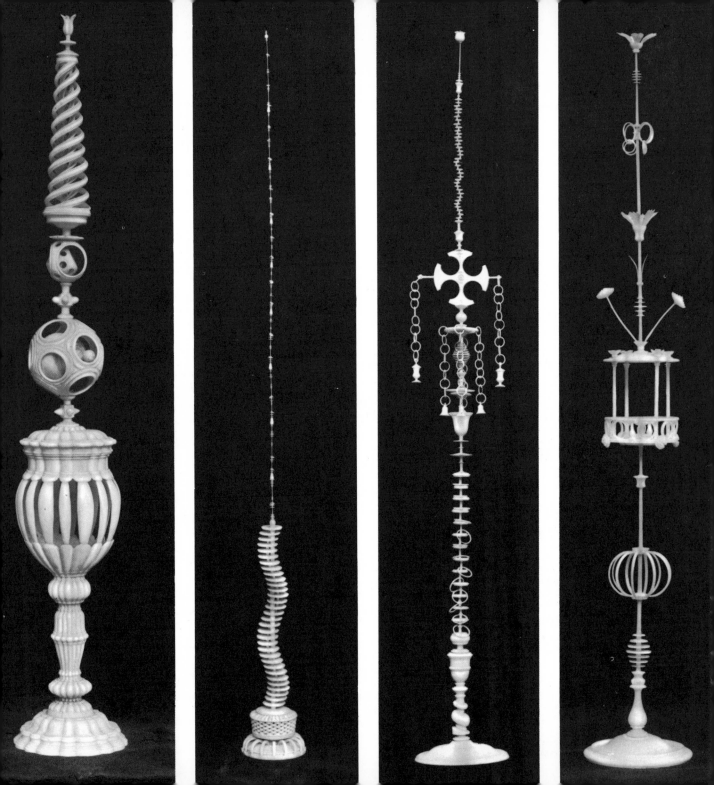

natural sciences. C. Heinrich, S. Zick, and J. Lücke made anatomical works: a skull, the organs of hearing, a foetus *in utero*, twins (Dresden, 1742), or sometimes curiosities of nature, such as Siamese brothers, or a bearded girl! We have mentioned powder-flasks, knobs for canes, and cutlery-handles; the birds and quadrupeds on the former remind one of those inside Mesopotamian bowls, arranged like revolving wheels and described by Parrot under the title of *Ibexes at the Spring*. On others we see strange faces, Turks, Roman Emperors, and composite figures [figures 122 and 123]. Logically enough, lions, dragons, and stag-hunting scenes form the designs on the handles of knives for cutting up the stag as often as they do on scent-bottles or curiously ornate beer mugs. These artifacts reached their peak at the beginning of the seventeenth century [figure 126].

This was not all. The Germans made balls fitting one inside the other, in the Chinese manner, and globes standing on high carved pedestals and used as magic lanterns [figures 113–116]. J. Teutschmann's crozier made up of manifold scrolls [figure 133], a masterpiece of rococo art, shows that this sort of work had developed along entirely new lines since the Gothic period. In a quite different genre, Nuremberg made a speciality of portable sundials [figure 117], derived from Roman originals. From the fifteenth and sixteenth centuries onwards, these were decorated with great splendour, using ivory, gilded bronze, and niello. Moreover, their usefulness was increased by adding a compass and numerous indications: a perpetual calendar, wind-rose, and longitudes of the chief European cities. It was an attempt to defeat the serious competition from pendulum clocks, and to persuade the public that the latter would never be satisfactory. The earliest ivory sundial belonged to Pope Paul III (Figdor Collection, Vienna, *c* 1464). Lastly, goldsmith-ivory carvers, such as Krüger and Köhler, added silver-gilt and enamel to small figures of beggars or representatives of various trades, such as cobblers, potters, etc, getting their inspiration from

117 Sundial (1629) by Conrad Karner of Nuremburg. The top opens perpendicularly, revealing on the four faces a compass, a wind-rose, the names of 18 European towns for which it was made, and lastly a calendar

113–116 (*opposite*) Chinese-influenced works of great virtuosity in the style of the Zick family of Nuremburg

P. J. Quast's engravings after Van Ostade. This genre was practised all over Europe, particularly in Italy, Spain, and Holland.

Germany did not, of course, possess a monopoly of ivory carving; Italy also had her professionals. We have mentioned Antonio Leoni, whose work is related to that of Elhafen and Permoser; Algardi belonged to his school. Renaissance Spain produced more wood-carving than ivory work, and there were many Frenchmen working there under Alonso Berruguete. In France, Van Opstal's Bacchanalian friezes [figure 118] must have been decorations for furniture, and Duquesnoy fashioned the children who have made him famous [figure 120], both in ivory and bronze.

We have already mentioned the Spanish passion for realism, taking the form of polychromatic figures of saints; their great sculptors, like Pedro de Mena, did not scorn the use of ivory. Like the Germans, the Spaniards excelled at anatomical interpretations, whether of children in statuettes of the Infant Christ [figure 136] or of men, for instance in

118 Bacchanalian scene by the Dutch artist Van Opstal (1595–1668), probably intended to decorate ebony furniture

120 *Sleeping Child* taken from a bronze by Duquesnoy (1594–1643), who was famous for this genre

Alonso Cano's *St Sebastian* [figure 121]. Microscopic reliefs were made both in Spain and Italy during the eighteenth century. This was a speciality of Ramon Capuz, born in Valencia in 1665, whose brother, a Dominican friar in the same town, also worked in ivory; he also made polychrome figures of ragged beggars. His work aroused so much admiration that Luis I, Prince of Asturias, wanted to learn his craft from him. In Italy, Bocenigo of Asti practised this genre, especially in the form of tobacco-jars. His work is very little known but can be seen in the museums of Asti and Turin, and the Louvre possesses a portrait-medallion of the Empress Marie-Louise in profile by him.

The most triumphant success in this genre of micro-relief was achieved by France in a whole series of charming little objects exemplifying the eighteenth-century rococo. German ivories showed their virility in innumerable objects for drinking, hunting, and war; French ivories were as feminine in their way, as the Gothic carvings exalting the Virgin or woman. Now they developed their airiest gifts to the service of woman by making a great number of objects for female use. We have already mentioned Diane de Poitiers' knife. Marie de Medicis' casket at Fontainebleau is decorated in a sober classical style [figure 124]. Duquesnoy and Van Opstal's reliefs in Rubens' vein display feminine attractions

122 German stag-hunting
knife handle, with a leonine
and satanic mask (with goat's
horns) above a heap of bones
symbolizing Hunger

123 German cane-handle of the 18th century

with unusual charm. Tobacco-graters were used by those women who habitually took snuff, but this widespread fashion had to be forbidden during Mass because the noise of grating tobacco made it impossible to hear the sermon. Spinning-wheels and spindles [figure 125] were used by women. Although, with a few exquisite exceptions [figure 128], tobacco-jars were seldom made of ivory and those preserved in museums are mostly of mother-of-pearl, lacquer, and Martin varnish (a form of copal varnish perfected in the eighteenth century by the Martin brothers) combined with gold, ivory was often used for powder and patch boxes.

Above all other accessories of feminine luxury, fans must be mentioned. We have referred above to their oriental and traditional design, based on the bunches of feathers still used in some countries. It is thought that in their present form they reached France about 1422, and England during the reign of Richard II; in *The Merry Wives of Windsor*

Shakespeare makes Falstaff say: 'When Mistress Bridget lost the handle of her fan'.

The custom of wearing a fan hooked onto the belt came from Italy and was particularly widespread at the court of Henri II and Catherine de Medicis. The fan consisted of a mount, and an upper part with the ribs covered in stuff or parchment; sometimes the parchment did not completely cover the ribs, the rest being decorated with scenes or medallions. Sometimes the upper part of the fan was composed entirely of pierced ribs making a sort of lattice-work, as in some Japanese fans, and one which belonged to Marie-Antoinette is decorated in this way with Roman soldiers fighting. The ornamentation of handles [figure 127] and graters went through several phases; under Louis XIV mythology was popular, under Louis XV charming rococo detail, under Louis XVI Venus and cupids.

In the decoration of these various objects, and the systematic development of the form of pierced work known as

125 The use of the lathe made it possible to create pieces as complicated as this spinning-wheel (French, 17th century)

126 A richly ornamented tankard and perfume flasks.
The tankard is decorated with a boar hunt, and the
perfume flasks with the pleasures of love and a garland
of putti (German, c 1700)

128 The delicacy of workmanship that had been achieved in ivory carving by the 18th century is clearly seen in this tobacco-jar, decorated with the taking of the Bastille

127 *(left)* French fan-case and shuttle from the 18th century

'mosaic', we must recognize the important influence of Dieppe. A text dated 1665 tells us that from 1384 onwards this town was importing large quantities of ivory *(morphi)* from West Africa, and after 1612 visitors from England or even Germany were amazed at the quality of the ivories to be seen at Dieppe, finding them 'superior to anything made elsewhere'. The Dieppe ivory carvers excelled in their fine art productions. Among these were allegorical groups, such as Belleteste's *Four Seasons* [figure 135], in the style of the statues in the park at Versailles; the flowing draperies and academic insistence on expression and symbolism are in contrast to the austerity of German pieces. In this class too

129 (left) Bi-valvular shell with Louis XV
ornamentation

130 and 131 Portrait medallion of A. Seba
(1727)

were medallions of the owner's names [figures 130 and
131], exquisite bi-valve shells in the rocaille style [figure
129] and compasses.

An unusual proof of the great vogue of ivory carving at
Dieppe is given us in Joseph Vernet's picture, *The Harbour
of Dieppe* (1765) [figure 134], where a pedlar is furtively
selling various objects from his basket in the middle of the
fish market, and carries a crucifix, one of the numerous
objects made at Dieppe. The practice of this art reached a
rare degree of perfection there, and has continued to the
present day, but during the last century it became a purely
commercial activity: 'I'm making one of my roses', the

132 *(left)* Beggar woman, Netherlands, 17th century. Astonishingly realistic figures representing beggars or trades were made throughout Europe in the 17th and 18th centuries in imitation of Chinese grotesques

133 *(opposite)* Episcopal crozier by Joseph Teutschmann (1717—1787)

modern craftsman will say, as if repeating a piece by heart or following a ready prepared sketch, rather than referring to nature.

Some of the makers of small objects at Dieppe were anonymous, and even if we do have textual evidence of their names, they often signed their works with 'marks' — an eye, or a hand — in imitation of medieval craftsmen. Another sign of the persistence of medieval tradition was their concentration on 'masterpieces'; this was the aim of the 'Compagnons du Devoir' in France. Thus eighteenth-century French work carried on the old traditions. This was the case in Germany, where goblets were reminiscent of the old drinking-horns, baroque altars of the old plaques or Carolingian book-covers, and in Italy, where the Renaissance found expression for the Roman tradition.

If we have laid stress on iconic objects, it is because the malleability of ivory is exceptionally favourable to trans-

135 *The Four Seasons*, a masterpiece of ivory carving from Dieppe, after the statues at Versailles; the artist, Jean-Antoine Belleteste (1731–1811), belonged to a family of ivory carvers

134 *(opposite)* Detail of *The Harbour at Dieppe* (1765) by J. Vernet, showing a pedlar selling ivory objects

lation into images. The study of ivories is particularly well-adapted to throw light on the highest aspirations of each country, each essential culture accentuating some primary symbolical theme. In France it was the triangle and woman (it is not without significance that the first link in a 'feminine' series found on her soil is the Venus of Lespugne, who is made up of triangles); in Italy, the tree; in Germany, the circle, symbol of masculinity. Nor was it unintentionally that we laid emphasis on the various vicissitudes passed through by the theme of the 'four beasts', the circular key-image of the West, and on the symbolical aspects of German baroque work. Thus it seems that the West did not ignore a language which is sometimes said to belong to primitive or traditional cultures alone.

136 Statuette of the infant Christ from Spain (late 17th century)